AERO SERIES   VOL. 32

THE
B-1
BOMBER

WILLIAM G. HOLDER

AERO
A division of TAB BOOKS Inc.
Blue Ridge Summit, PA 17214

358.42

12-86 M1 500
FIRST EDITION
FIRST PRINTING

Copyright © 1986 by TAB BOOKS Inc.
Printed in the United States of America

Library of Congress Cataloging in Publication Data

Holder, William G., 1937-
The B1 bomber.

(Aero series ; vol. 32)
Includes index.
1. B-1 bomber.   I. Title.   II. Title: B-one bomber.
UG1242.B6H644   1986   358.4'2   85-27634
ISBN 0-8168-0613-6 (pbk.)

CONTENTS

ACKNOWLEDGMENTS

Major George Peck, B-1 Public Affairs Officer
Mike Levy, Aeronautical Systems Division Historical Officer
Helen Kavanaugh and Gene Hollingsworth, ASD Public Affairs Office
Len Pytel and Tom Mayenshein—Artwork Support
The Boeing Company
Rockwell International Company
Cindy Andes—typing
Glenn Holder—editing
Lt. Stan VenderWerf—editing

FOREWORD

General William E. Thurman

Since its rebirth in 1981 the B-1B has emerged as one of the most exciting programs in the Air Force today. It is a program that has broken new ground on several fronts. As America's premier strategic long-range weapon system, it brings together a host of new technologies such as the AN/ALQ-161 defensive avionics. The world's most advanced electronic protection system, the Eaton-built "electronic umbrella," allows the B-1B to penetrate the most heavily defended areas with relative impunity. An advanced radar design gives the swing-wing bomber unprecedented weapon delivery accuracy and the ability to terrain-follow at treetop levels and bullet speeds. The solid, dependable General Electric F-101 engines exploit turbojet technology to insure the new bomber has the guts and the gas to get to crisis spots anywhere on the globe. Smart engineering by the Rockwell airframe people has given the B-1B an ever decreasing radar cross section, tremendously complicating the job of anyone who would defend against it.

All in all, the B-1B is a technical marvel blending available technology with state-of-the-art breakthroughs to produce an airplane high in capability yet low in technical risk—in short, an airplane that is affordable, maintainable, and reliable, yet potent enough to serve as a true deterrent.

The technology front, however, isn't the only one breached by the Air Force-led B-1B team. The team has also taken the initiative on the business front. Our challenge from the beginning was to build the most capable bomber in the world sooner and cheaper than many people thought possible. Our byword was innovation. For only through innovation could we build the B-1B for $20.5 billion (in 1981 dollars) and put 100 of the aircraft on the ramp, ready for full operation by 1988.

We are meeting the challenge by taking a hard-headed business approach. Our first order of business was to take charge—literally. The Air Force's Aeronautical Systems Division stepped up to the task with the B-1B System Program Office. It was to serve as "prime contractor" overseeing the effort of four associate contractors: Rockwell International's North American Aviation Operations for airframe and integration, Boeing Military Airplane Company for offensive avionics and controls and displays, Eaton Corporations' AIL Division for defensive avionics, and General Electric's Aircraft Engine Business Group for the engines to power the bomber. This team approach with the Air Force in the lead is proving to be a real cost saver.

Multiyear procurement was another common sense approach we took. By buying the last 82 aircraft under one contract, we expect to save over $1 billion through economic ordering of raw materials, longer parts runs resulting in few start-up costs and savings accrued through minimizing the impact of inflation.

The acronym SAIP stands for another innovative program we've initiated to buy our spare parts during the initial production run. SAIP, or Spares Acquisition Integrated with Production, capitalizes on the inherent efficiencies of an established production run. It allows us to sock away spare parts for a rainy day at prices that will bring back the sunshine for the hard-pressed American taxpayer.

Tech Mod, short for Technology Modernization, is another innovation where up-front investment to modernize plant facilities and processes mean long-term cost avoidance. It not only lowers costs but, perhaps more importantly, helps build an American industrial base that is more competitive and makes future weapons systems more affordable as well.

But this is only part of the story. I hope that this fine book will give you a better appreciation of the B-1B program: what it was—what it will be. In many ways the B-1B is typically American. Like our people, it is enormously complex yet enormously capable: it is beautiful to behold, yet threatened by none.

The B-1B is truly America's airplane.

WILLIAM E. THURMAN
Major General, USAF
Deputy for B-1B

Chapter I

ROOTS

It's really difficult to know where to start the story of the B-1 bomber. Even a skilled genealogist might have trouble determining the correct developmental lines to reach the apex of the B-1 family tree.

Although there have been numerous offshoots and alternative proposals down through the years, the goal of each remained the same—to eventually replace the venerable B-52, which had gone out of production in 1962. At the rate the proposals were progressing toward flight hardware during the 1950s and '60s, it appeared that the B-52 might well have to be flying to the year 2062 before a replacement aircraft could be designed and fielded.

The B-1 story probably starts, though, in 1955 with the initial requirement (GOR 82) to design a "chemically-powered, strategic bombardment reconnaissance weapon system 110A/L." Contracts were let to both Boeing and North American Aviation to conduct the initial studies. What would eventually evolve from GOR 82 would be the giant delta-wing B-70 bomber.

In 1957, North American would be selected as the prime contractor for the advanced new system. The first flight would come seven years later in 1964. But pressures of various types on the B-70 would eventually kill the program after only two of the giant planes were produced.

Opponents of the majestic plane argued that strategic deterrence could be better served by intercontinental ballistic missiles or air-launched missiles. There was also the possibility of a version of the C-5 transport being equipped with long-range missiles to fulfill the strategic need. It would be an argument which would continue to be waged well into the 1970s and '80s, during the time periods of the two eventual B-1 programs.

North American B-70 Valkyrie Chronology

22 March 1955
Initial Requirement (GOR 82)

8 November 1955
Letter contract issued to Boeing ($4,550,000) and North American ($1,000,000) to furnish a design for a chemically-powered, strategic bombardment reconnaissance Weapon System 110A/L, furnish models, drawings, specifications, reports, and other data as well as conduct studies and wind tunnel tests and put together a mock-up. The mock-up was to be completed and ready for Air Force inspection within 2 years of the date on which the contractor accepted the contract. Contractor fees were not to exceed $450,000.

15 March 1956
Definitive Phase I type of letter contract with Boeing for Weapon System 110A/L. Total estimated cost: $19,943,966. (Subject to renegotiation)

15 March 1956
Definitive Phase I type of letter contract with North American for Weapon System 110A/L. Total estimated cost: $9,999,972. (Subject to renegotiation)

August 1957
Air Force granted authority to commit a total of $12,000,000 of FY 58 P-600 money to the B-70 program, $2,000,000 each to be paid to Boeing and North American to cover costs incurred between 1 July—31 December 1957, the balance to be provided to the winner of the evaluation of the Phase I effort.

December 1957
Near the end of December 1957, North American selected by the Source Selection Board. The Fiscal Year 1958 budget calls for spending approximately $90,000,000 for work on the aircraft and its General Electric powerplant.

23 December 1957*
Production Decision

---

*Reoriented to experimental program, 1 December 1959—development of major subsystems deferred.   Two XB-70's and 180-hour test program approved by DOD in 1964.

B-1 isn't a unique designation for a U.S. military aircraft; this early bird also carried the same name.
(U.S. Air Force Museum photo)

The bomber that had to be replaced. These B-52s are shown on the flight line at Kelly Air Force Base, Texas. The last of the venerable old Stratofortresses were built in 1962, and a number of them could still be flying at the end of the century.
(U.S. Air Force photo)

26 January 1959
HQ USAF announced availability of $5,000,-
000 of FY 60 funds to support an experimental
model of a bombing navigation subsystem.

21 September 1964
First Flight

March 1967
Beginning of Phase Out—Project transferred
to NASA. Phase Out completed with transfer to
XB-70A (No. 1) to Air Force Museum.**

But there were many other ideas on follow-on
bomber aircraft concepts being kicked around
during those 1960s years. The list of acronyms
might sound like the element of some secret
code, but they were really much less exotic.
SLAB...ERSA...LAMP...AMP...AMPSS...
AMSA. The abbreviations really stood for the
many studies that considered alternatives for
replacing the B-52.

The studies probably started mostly because
of the concern military strategists felt after one
of the Air Force's U-2 spy planes had been shot
down by a Soviet surface-to-air missile while
flying at extremely high altitudes over Russia
in 1960. The U-2 incident forced planners to re-
examine the then-prevalent bomber philosophy of a stable high-altitude platform performing well above the range of conventional anti-
aircraft weapons. The emergence of an operational radar-guided SAM made such tactics
suspect because of the ease of targeting large
bombers, which by design were not very ma-
neuverable.

Radar's weakest point of detection was near
the ground because its beams are "line of
sight," and the energy cannot go over-or-
around obstacles such as natural terrain to
detect an object, like a low-flying bomber. This
led planners to the obvious conclusion that the
best way to reach enemy targets in the future
was by penetrating hostile airspace at

**XB-70A (No. 2) lost in mid-air collision w/F-104, 8 June 1966—flew 32 minutes at Mach 3 on 19 May 1966.

The B-70 was the initial attempt to replace the B-52. The giant delta-wing bomber evolved as a result of a 1955 study. The first flight of the majestic machine came in 1964. Only two were built, with the only remaining example now on display at the Air Force Museum at Wright-Patterson Air Force Base, Ohio. (U.S. Air Force photo)

Rockwell International (then North American Aviation) studied many different and varied configurations before the final AMSA and B-1 shape was achieved.

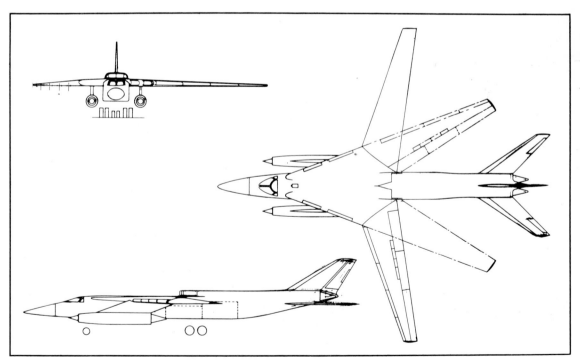

One of the very early AMSA configuration concepts. Note the forward position of the two engines and the extremely large swing wings. The final B-1 configuration would bear little resemblance to this particular concept. (U.S. Air Force drawing)

This AMSA design proposal was submitted by General Dynamics. The artist's concept shows the plane in low-level flight with wings retracted in the rearward position. The engines are mounted in pairs far back on the fuselage. The design also features a high wing mounting. (General Dynamics drawing)

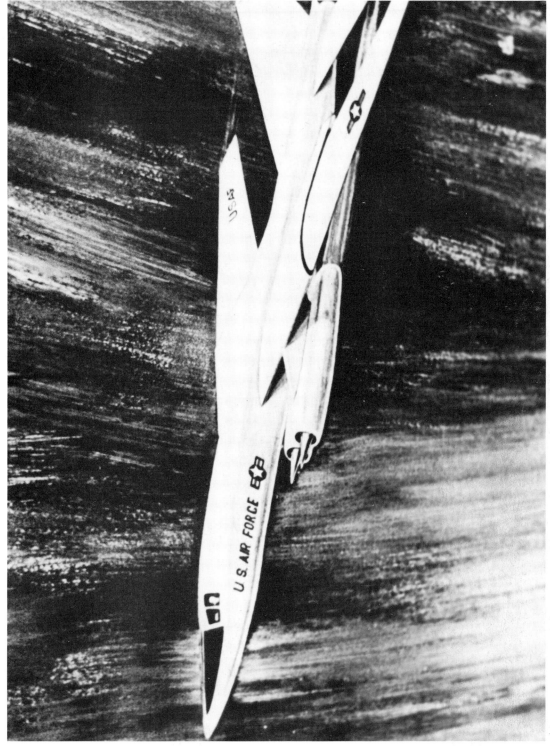

Another of the early AMSA concepts. This particular configuration sports four engines mounted close to the fuselage in B-52 type engine pods.
(U.S. Air Force drawing)

This later AMSA design shows some similarity to the final B-1. Its characteristics include far aft engine locations and high-mounted wing: a major portion of the wing is fixed with only the outer portions being of variable geometry. (U.S. Air Force drawing)

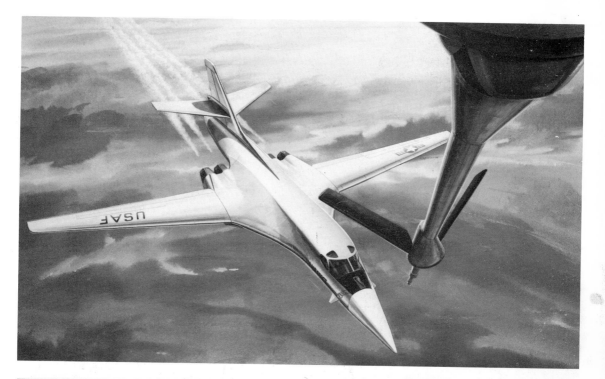

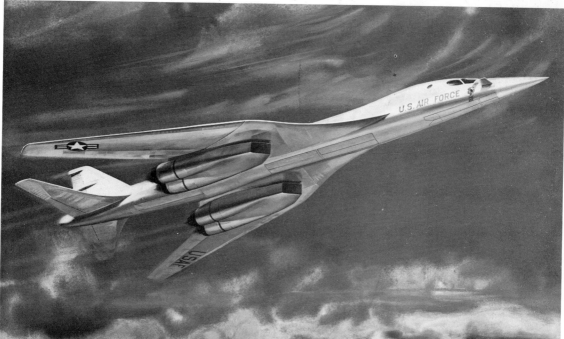

These 1970 artists' concepts began to show the AMSA (it was also being called the B-1) as the final configuration would appear. These sketches show the small vanes on the front of the fuselage and the mounting of the engines in the approximate location they would rest in the B-1 configuration.

(U.S. Air Force drawings)

It looked real, but it was made mostly of wood. The initial B-1 mockup proved to be of great benefit to the Air Force in evaluating the locations and functioning of various systems. (North American Rockwell photo)

North American Rockwell also built this full-scale pivot mockup. The pivot and wing operated through the full design swing arc, and all areas of interest were covered with Plexiglas to allow observation while the pivot system was operating. (North American Rockwell photo)

extremely low altitudes and high speeds. It's a philosophy that is still standing in good stead in the 1980s.

The first study, carried out in 1961, was called the SLAB project, for Subsonic Low Altitude Bomber. Then came the ERSA (Extended Range Strategic Aircraft) and the LAMP (Low-Altitude Manned Penetrator) studies, which were carried out in 1963. The LAMP design was to be a 350,000-pound craft capable of being armed with "laydown" weapons.

That same year, two other key studies were started, the AMP (Advanced Manned Penetrator) and the AMPSS (Advanced Manned Penetrating Strategic Systems.)

In the AMP effort, the Air Force requirements called for a preliminary design and evaluation of four different concepts: (1) all subsonic low-altitude, (2) subsonic low altitude with high altitude medium supersonic capability, (3) subsonic low altitude with a high altitude, high supersonic capability, and (4) vertical/short takeoff and landing vehicle. AMPSS was a study to optimize the subsonic low altitude aircraft with a high altitude medium supersonic capability.

The AMP and AMPSS studies ended in 1965, and were followed later in the year by the well known AMSA (Advanced Manning Strategic Aircraft) studies, which continued into early 1969. The AMSA program called for five

Also built was a full-scale mockup of the crew escape capsule, which can be clearly seen resting near the back wall in this photo. (U.S. Air Force photo)

Several different versions of the General Dynamics F-111 swing-wing aircraft would come into play during the B-1 program. Versions of the aircraft were considered prior to the initial B-1 program. After that program was curtailed, stretched versions of the F-111 were examined as possible alternatives to the B-1B. Neither, though, ever came to fruition.

(General Dynamics photo)

supplementary studies: (1) a propulsion study; (2) an alternate armament loading study; (3) a reliability study, (4) a titanium cost study, and (5) a maintainability study.

Within the AMSA study effort was a long list of separate study tasks, such as: crew factors, limited war analysis, enduring survivability, survivability and vulnerability, design trade studies, and bomber decoy missle analysis.

AMSA studies progressed quickly, to the point where the Air Force was prepared to initiate contract definition in 1967. However, then-Secretary of Defense Robert McNamara still

had reservations about the effectiveness of a manned bomber in the "missile age." Appearing before Congress in 1966, he talked about an aircraft armed with long-range missiles and the manned bomber as a supplement to the ballistic missile. He supported a strategic version of the F-111A aircraft, in contrast to the Air Force, which regarded such an aircraft as an interim AMSA system. The irony of President Carter's decision to cancel production of the B-1 some 11 years later and proceed with the cruise missile, was, in fact, the solution that Secretary McNamara had favored at this time.

The AMSA concept was the direct predecessor to the B-1, and led to the Air Force RFP (Request for Proposal) to industry for the B-1 in December 1969. The AMSA had become the B-1. After nearly seven months of evaluation, Rockwell was selected to build the B-1 with General Electric providing the F101 turbofan engines.

After nearly 14 years of careful planning and study by the best brains in the Department of Defense, the Air Force and the aerospace industry, the B-1 was reality.

It is no wonder that someone said that AMSA really stood for " . . . America's Most Studied Aircraft."

In October of 1971, the first full-scale mock-up of the fledgling B-1 bomber was completed and approved. It appeared that everything was on a roll for the "Bomber of the Century," but that's getting ahead of the story. Rough waters were ahead.

The next chapter, though, takes a look at the first of the B-1's, now referred to as the B-1A, an aircraft whose time would never come to pass.

Chapter II
THE FIRST B-1

The B-1 program received undoubtedly the highest priority ever accorded any new Air Force system. So much was expected of the new bomber that pressure for success was immense. The aircraft represented a quantum jump in technology for the many new jobs it would be required to perform.

With its variably geometry wings and high thrust-to-weight ratio, the B-1 would be able to use shorter runways, a characteristic that could enable the plane to be easily dispersed across the country. The plane was to have a lower turn-around time, including methods for rapidly checking out and verifying its advanced subsystems. The new bomber would be able to get away from bases more quickly because the plane's smaller size reduced the required takeoff interval between aircraft.

Supersonic fly-out speed would get the plane airborne faster, a distinct advantage in a nuclear environment. Near-sonic performance on the deck would enable the advanced plane to penetrate sophisticated defense networks. And finally, the plane's extremely small radar cross section would minimize its detection.

Add all those advantages to the fact that the plane could also deliver a much larger payload of missiles and bombs, and the advantages of such an aircraft were evident. At least, these were the arguments the Air Force had used to convince the President and Congress that such an aircraft was needed. The question now remained as to whether the plane that would evolve would be able to deliver.

The program was never without its criticizers. And throughout its development time period of the early 1970s, the future of the B-1 development would be consistently threatened.

The B-1 program formally began in July of 1970, when Rockwell International was awarded the prime contract and General Electric was given the engine go-ahead. Competition had been heated for the lucrative award with Boeing and General Dynamics submitting counter bids for the overall system contract. Pratt and Whitney had been the only contractor bidding for the propulsion system.

The initial B-1 schedule called for a Preliminary Design Review to be held in July of 1971, with the first flight tagged for April 1974. The production decision would then be made a year later with the first production aircraft supposedly being available in October of 1977. Two years after that date, the B-1 was projected to be operational with the Strategic Air Command.

The 241 B-1's were projected with an unheard-of 13,500-hour lifetime, with a considerable portion of that time being spent at high speeds and low altitudes. Optimism was high for the new system, but so were the awesome requirements it was being asked to meet.

Although different in some areas, all of the competing B-1 design proposals had featured movable wings as the optimum solution for fulfilling the requirements that had been laid on the aircraft. It was apparent to the designers that to accomplish both low altitude and supersonic penetration missions with a short take-off capability, the swing wing was the only way to go.

For its time, the B-1 was definitely pushing the technology to the hilt. Every aspect of the new plane represented new challenges to the aerodynamicist, the propulsion specialist, and the military planner. An examination of those technologies that made up this "first of a breed" follows.

Aerodynamics

The blended wing-body configuration was one of the first noticeable aspects of the plane's advanced design. The arrangement afforded high aerodynamic efficiency and was structurally efficient, allowing the swing wing concept to be utilized. It would be a configuration that would be used again later in the F-16 Fighting Falcon fighter, which was also in early design during the same time period.

Previous experience with the swing-wing F-111 had provided data for the B-1's swing wing. But much development work was required since studies had shown wing loadings of over 200 pounds/square foot at a full fuel load condition with the wings in the full-forward position. In that forward position the span was 136.7 feet, and while retracted fully in the supersonic position, the span was reduced considerably to only 78.2 feet.

But in the straight position, the wings weren't really straight, i.e., perpendicular to the B-1 fuselage. In that "low-and-slow position," the leading edge was still slightly swept at 15 degrees, while the value soared to 67.5 degrees in the fully-retracted position.

With a large percentage of the B-1's flights targeted for low altitude conditions, there was concern about high crew fatigue for long periods of flight in turbulent air. Enter the small vanes located on the front of the B-1's fuselage. These devices served as aerodynamic shock absorbers during flight, minimizing the continuous oscillations that would be felt by the crew.

Called the Low Altitude Ride Control System at the time, the system could suppress both up and down motions. The lower rudder panel provides sideway motion suppression, and could be activiated by sensors in the fuselage.

The B-1's smokeless engines meet and surpass the emission standards set for 1976 automobiles.

The B-1, in subsonic cruise, produces no more pollutants per mile than two automobiles cruising at 60 mph.

The B-1 operating without afterburner on climbout is quieter than a B-52.

Over 40 years of manufacturing COST-CONSCIOUS EXPERIENCE has gone into the B-1. Here is the proof:

The blended wing-body configuration of the B-1 is clearly visible as this B-1 prototype takes to the air. Note the large wing flaps.   (U.S. Air Force photo)

B-1 prototype 40158, the first constructed, kicks up a little smoke on a landing at Edwards Air Force Base in this 1975 photo. (U.S. Air Force photo)

B-1 MATERIALS
AV-1

	% OF DCPR WT
ALUMINUM	41.3
STEEL	6.6
TITANIUM	21.0
COMPOSITES	.3
FIBERGLASS	
POLYIMIDE	30.8
QUARTZ	
OTHERS	

This drawing shows the various materials used in the original B-1. Over 41 percent of the aircraft weight was aluminum. That amount had been increased earlier in the program by reducing the amount of titanium. (U.S. Air Force drawing)

First B-58—55 man-hours per pound
First F-15—31 man-hours per pound
First B-1—27.8 man-hours per pound

Advances in technology from the B-52 to the B-1 far exceed those advances experienced on the transition from props to jets.

The B-1, in terms of initial cost, cost of ownership, and total mission performance, is the most economical solution to modernizing the manned bomber force.

Cost-effective longevity: proof load tests show the B-1 airframe is so durable that present Air Force cadets who may eventually fly the airplane will be eligible for retirement before the end of the B-1's operational lifetime.

Every heartbeat of the B-1 is monitored in real time on the ground allowing instantaneous decisions between ground control and the flight crew during conduct of each flight test task based on data rather than guesswork.

The B-1 swing wing allows quick short-field takeoffs (wings forward) and a smooth high-speed penetration at very low levels (wings aft).

The B-1 electrical multiplex subsystem replaces a quarter of a million feet of wire. That's half a ton of wire per airplane.

In penetrating at sea level, the B-1, carrying twice the load of a B-52 at a speed 50 percent faster, uses appreciably less fuel.

Before the first B-1 test flight in 1974, the GE F101 turbofan powerplant was tested at Arnold Engineering Development Center. The engine passed its Preliminary Flight Rating Test after approximately 80 hours of altitude testing at Arnold and 60 hours of endurance running at GE's plant near Cincinnati. *(U.S. Air Force photo)*

The highest thrust levels recorded in 25 years of jet engine testing at the Arnold Center were attained during the 1976 testing of the 30,000-pound thrust F101 B-1 engine. The tests were run in one of the high-altitude test cells of the center's Engine Test Facility.(U.S. Air Force photo)

This wall of instruments and panels greeted the flight crews of the B-1 prototypes. Notice the tight quarters for the pilot and copilot in this arrangement. (U.S. Air Force photo)

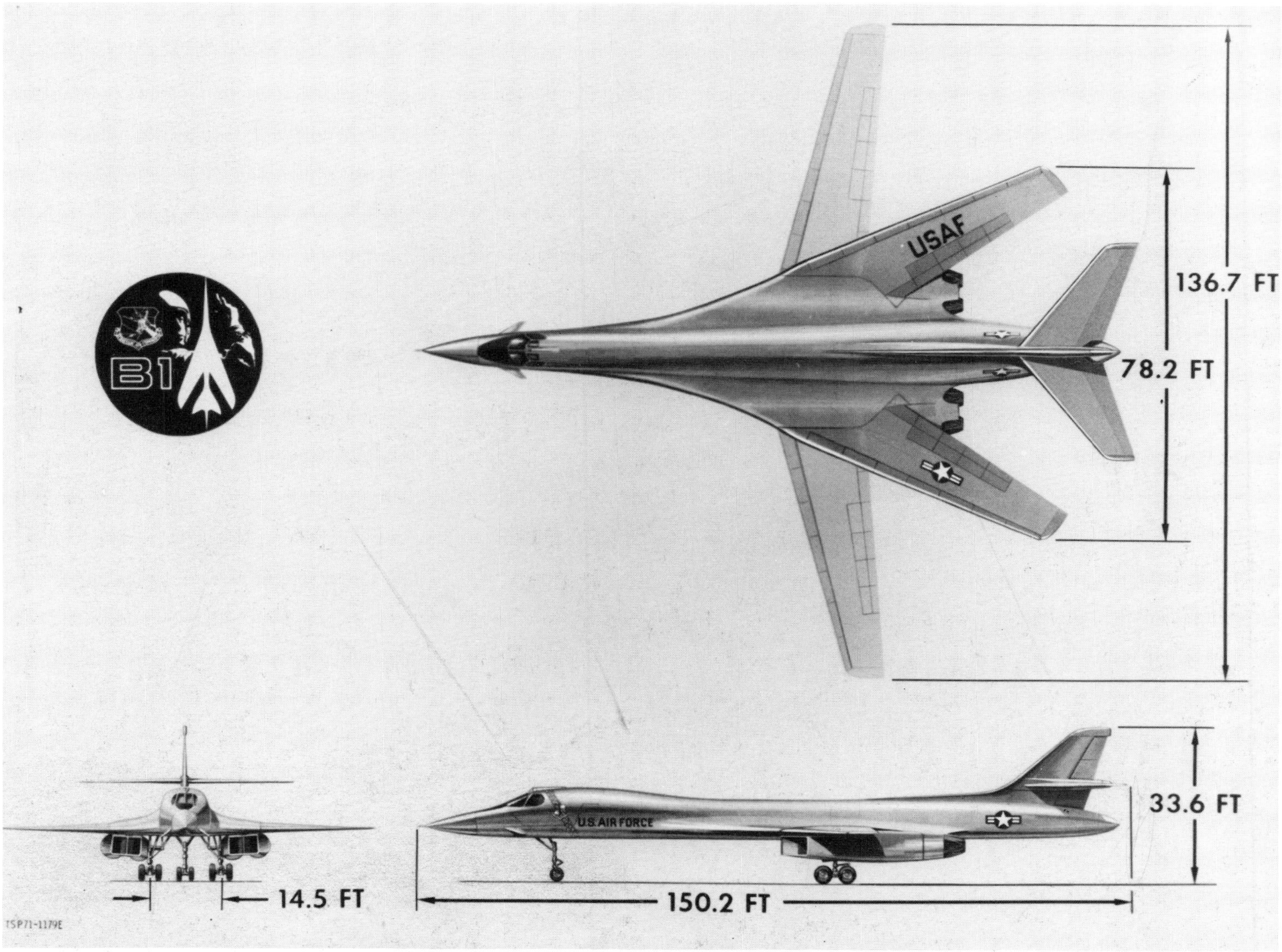

An early drawing of the initial B-1 design. The initial prototype aircraft ended up looking very much like this sketch. (U.S. Air Force photo)

136.7 FT

78.2 FT

33.6 FT

150.2 FT

14.5 FT

USAF

U.S. AIR FORCE

B1

A 1971 North American Rockwell artist's concept of the B-1 presented very accurately the final configuration of the aircraft. The drawing shows the bomber traversing rough terrain at low altitude, a capability it would retain throughout its stormy development period.

(North American Rockwell photo)

The B-1, second to none, is the world's fastest heavy bomber, with the biggest payload and greatest range.

The B-1 is hard to find even within a dense radar environment. With more than twice the performance of the B-52 it is many times smaller on a radar screen—if you can see it.

In 25 flights and nearly 120 hours of "safety first" flying time, there has not been a single incident that put either the aircraft or the crew in jeopardy.

The B-1 proved its compatibility with the KC-135 tanker on only its sixth flight, and in-flight refueling has been a part of every subsequent test flight.

It's not surprising the B-1 flight test record is

outstanding: it had more than 100,000 laboratory test hours behind it before its first take-off.

The GE engines developed for the B-1 have already accumulated nearly 9,000 test hours.

The B-1 has been performing reliably and durably. It flew three missions, each in excess of 6 hours, in a space of only 10 working days.

A SAC operational pilot flew the B-1 for evaluation on the 16th test flight (Maj. George Larson SAC/AFTEC). He performed the tasks routinely, including aerial refueling.

The B-1 keeps tabs on itself. Its on-board central integrated test system is constantly scanning the aircraft's systems and gives crewmembers an up-to-the-second status report during flight.

The B-1 airfoil section was a unique aerodynamic design specifically tailored for the B-1, enabling it to attain a near-peak efficiency for the widely diverse conditions of takeoff and landing, subsonic cruise at high lift, low altitude penetration at low lift, and supersonic penetration at moderate lift levels.

Structure/Materials

With the Mach 2 sustained performance that was projected for the B-1, aerodynamic heating bcame a prime design consideration. The maximum temperature in the 300 degree range initially caused engineers to consider using a high percentage of titanium in the structure.

The titanium usage was also needed for the Mach 1.2 low-level dash capability that had been specified during the AMSA studies. That requirement, however, was reduced because of the inability of the crew to detect and identify targets adequately at such high speeds so close to the ground. With strength requirements reduced, engineers saw the opportunity to use more aluminum in the B-1 structure.

Titanium had originally been listed as constituting 40 percent of the structure. After the performance reduction, only half that amount of titanium was used, with over 40 percent being aluminum and 16 percent being steel.

A noticeable effect of the titanium/aluminum switch was the change in location of the horizontal tail. Originally set low on the fuselage near the hot engine exhaust, the tail was moved farther up on the vertical stabilizer.

All the B-1's external surfaces were fabricated

1974 structural testing at the Lockheed proof load facility at Palmdale tested to 100 percent of design limits the aircraft was expected to encounter in operational service. All types of maneuvers were simulated in the testing, which included low-level flight, approach and landing, and ground taxi maneuvering. (U.S. Air Force photo)

One of four B-1 air inlets is shown assembled with the engine to which it will supply air prior to 1974 subsonic tests at the Arnold Engineering Development Center. Some five months of testing was accomplished on the engine/inlet combination to ensure their proper operation throughout the bomber's speed range. *(U.S. Air Force photo)*

In a 1975 test, a full-scale model of the B-1 covered with a brass screen and sheet metal served as an electronic test bed. Tests performed on this setup included those to ensure that the bomber's multiple antennas would operate properly in their locations without mutual interference. *(U.S. Air Force photo)*

B-1 MATERIALS

- ALUMINUM
- TITANIUM
- STEEL
- PLASTICS

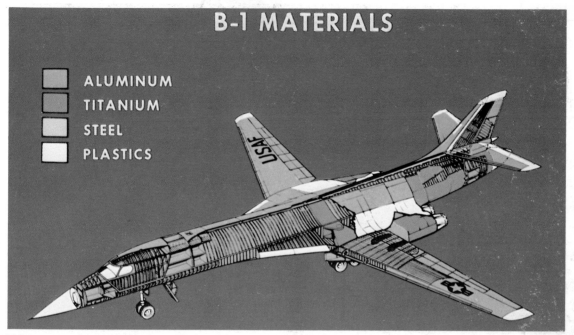

This cutaway of the initial B-1A model shows the various materials planned for the aircraft. The B-1B would eventually use much of the same material selection. (U.S. Air Force photo)

On several occasions during the B-1's lifetime, the F-111/FB-111 or proposed variants of it have been considered as either replacements or supplements to the B-1. Shown is the unbuilt FB-111H in artist's conception. (U.S. Air Force photo)

Crew escape capsule in testing. The concept was found to be very limited in its application and was dropped in favor of ejection seats.
(U.S. Air Force photo)

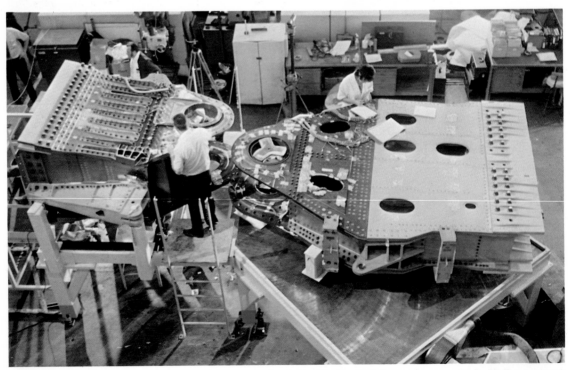

Hinge mechanism for B-1A swing wing under construction in the Rockwell plant.
(U.S. Air Force photo)

Number two B-1A prototype on the flight apron at Edwards Air Force Base. This aircraft would later be used in the B-1B flight test program for structural loads testing work. (U.S. Air Force photo)

Inflight refueling of one of the B-1A prototypes from a KC-135 tanker. (U.S. Air Force photo)

B-1A prototype during period of flight testing operations, 1981.   (U.S. Air Force photo)

The three B-1A prototypes during the flight testing period of the 1970s. The first production B-1A would eventually join the fleet after the B-1A program was cancelled. (U.S. Air Force photos)

B-1A prototype number three received a desert camouflage scheme, the only B-1 so painted. Production B-1Bs would be delivered in European One paint scheme. (U.S. Air Force photos)

Loading operations of the SRAM missile onto B-1A. The B-1B will also carry this weapon as well as the air-launched cruise missile.

(U.S. Air Force photos)

Mating of fuselage sections of first production B-1B.   (U.S. Air Force photo)

Wing mating operations of first production B-1B.   (U.S. Air Force photo)

B-1 prototype 40158 first sees the light of day at the Palmdale manufacturing facility. The bomber would never evolve to operational status in this configuration, but this aircraft and the other two flying prototypes would serve as the basis for the new aircraft that would follow.

(U.S. Air Force photo)

Aerial refueling compatibility with existing KC-135 tanker aircraft was a requirement for the B-1. That capability was tested and proved on many occasions, one of which is shown here. The location of the B-1's refueling probe is clearly visible on the nose, directly in front of the windscreen. *(U.S. Air Force photo)*

of aluminum as were the internal structures. The in-board end of the wing, the carry-through assembly, and certain aft fuselage sections used titanium.

Obviously, an area of great concern, material-wise, was the wing pivoting area. That so-important steel pin—which had to sustain the massive loads during the wing rotation process—actually consisted of two pins, one inside the other.

The unique design allowed for failure of one pin without impairing the functioning of the

wing. The B-1 design requirement actually called for the wing-moving hydraulic system to be capable of moving a one million pound load.

Engines

The choice of the B-1 engines was dictated by unrefueled intercontinental range, Mach 2 performance, and high thrust. The General Electric F101 engine proved to be an excellent match for those tough requirements.

Origins of the engine went back to the late 1960s and the AMSA deliberations. Testing of the engine's major components began in 1970 with the contract go-ahead coming the same year.

The original F101 was a compact two-shaft, ducted afterburning turbofan with a variable-area convergent-divergent nozzle. The engine had a full-length by-pass duct which carried the fan slipstream air around the outside of the core engine to fuel spray bars and flame holders adjacent to the turbine exhaust stream.

The engine had a 2:1 bypass ratio, i.e., one-third of the outside air passed into the core engine and two-thirds moved down by bypass duct. The takeoff thrust rating of the engine was about 17,000 pounds. That figure was increased substantially with afterburning to 30,000 pounds. Mass flow for the 181-inch long, 55-inch diameter, 4,000 pound power-plant was about 350 pounds per minute.

With a pair of the engines located in each of two widely-separated pods, there was initial concern on the consequences of an engine-out situation. It was later determined, though, that with the help of the plane's advanced flight control system, any propulsion-related contingency could be handled.

Extensive full-scale engine tests were performed at the Air Force's Arnold Engineering Development Center (AEDC), integrating the new engine with the B-1 airframe and measuring the effectiveness of the engine/inlet combination.

AEDC would also be involved in numerous other aspects of the aircraft's development. B-1 tests at the Tennessee facility also included verification of the crew escape capsule, the small forward aerodynamic fins, the Short Range Attack Missile (SRAM), and studies of the B-1 delivering that missile.

Hydraulic System

From the hydraulic system point of view, the original B-1 was a highly-redundant aircraft.

Two large pumps per engine supplied four completely separate systems and were used for all movable control surfaces. One system could have been lost without compromising the plane's overall effectiveness, and even two could go down without having to abort the mission. Reliability was definitely a keynote in the basic design of the B-1.

Avionics

The B-1's world of avionics integration consisted of some 130 "black boxes" all working closely together. The system was compared this way: If the aircraft and engines were the muscle and bone of the new bomber, then the avionics were its eyes, brains, and nerves.

There were actually two separate avionics integration tasks being performed on the B-1. The offensive avionics segment enabled very accurate navigation and the placement of the weapons on the target. The offensive systems operator controlled that operation. The defensive avionics segment included the electronic countermeasures (jammers) and expendable countermeasures (flares, chaff) that enhanced the survivability of the B-1 in penetrating hostile territories.

Hardware-wise, the major offensive and defensive avionics sensor elements were: Litton inertial measurement units, the Texas Instrument terrain-following radar, the General Electric forward-looking radar, the Hughes Aircraft forward-looking infrared (FLIR) sensor, a Singer-Kearfott doppler radar, Honeywell radar altimeters, and the AIL radio frequency surveillance sensor.

The most significant offensive controls and displays include three cathode ray tubes for data display, a multi-function display for displaying the forward-looking infrared, a forward-looking radar screen, a data entry unit which allowed the operator to enter new flight programs, and a keyboard which permitted entry of new data into the avionics control unit complex.

With the flexibility of carrying either eight

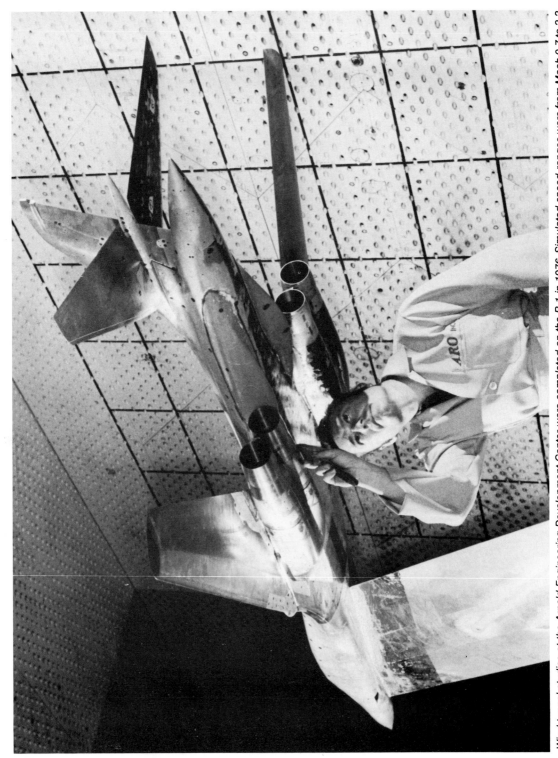

Wind tunnel studies at the Arnold Engineering Development Center were completed on the B-1 in 1976. Simulated speed ranges were from Mach 0.7 to 2.2. The effects of a redesigned aft radar housing were also examined. (U.S. Air Force photo)

The fleet of three B-1 flying prototypes. The planned number had been larger, but due to cost considerations, was reduced to three. These aircraft would continue to fly in a research mode even after the B-1 production contract was cancelled in 1977. Later, they would be modified to support the B-1B program. (U.S. Air Force photo)

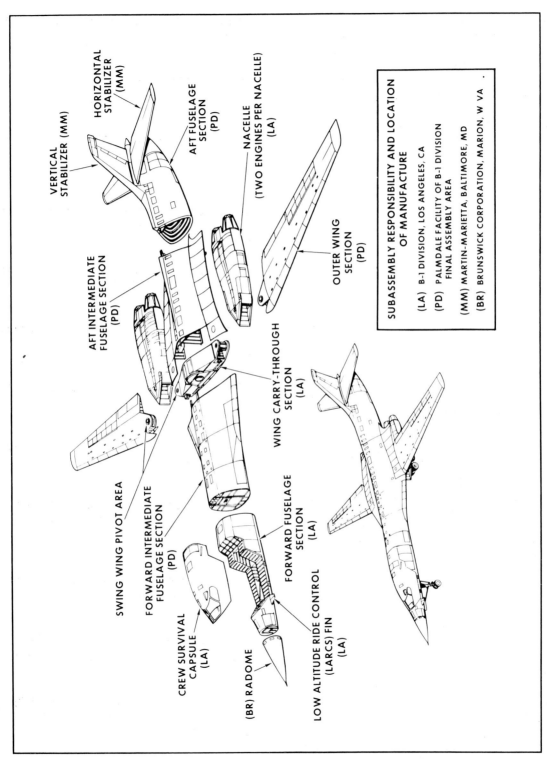

VERTICAL STABILIZER (MM)

HORIZONTAL STABILIZER (MM)

AFT FUSELAGE SECTION (PD)

NACELLE (TWO ENGINES PER NACELLE) (LA)

AFT INTERMEDIATE FUSELAGE SECTION (PD)

OUTER WING SECTION (PD)

SWING WING PIVOT AREA

WING CARRY-THROUGH SECTION (LA)

FORWARD INTERMEDIATE FUSELAGE SECTION (PD)

FORWARD FUSELAGE SECTION (LA)

CREW SURVIVAL CAPSULE (LA)

(BR) RADOME

LOW ALTITUDE RIDE CONTROL (LARCS) FIN (LA)

SUBASSEMBLY RESPONSIBILITY AND LOCATION OF MANUFACTURE

(LA) B-1 DIVISION, LOS ANGELES, CA
(PD) PALMDALE FACILITY OF B-1 DIVISION FINAL ASSEMBLY AREA
(MM) MARTIN-MARIETTA, BALTIMORE, MD
(BR) BRUNSWICK CORPORATION, MARION, W VA .

B-1 subassemblies; note that the four main subassemblies were fabricated in four different locations. This drawing shows the escape module, which would later be dropped from the model.
(North American Rockwell drawing)

SRBMs, or a combination of SRBMs and nuclear gravity weapons or conventional high-explosive weapons, the offensive avionics system and the crew had the option of selecting automatic weapon delivery as required to achieve the mission objectives.

Among the main elements at the defensive operator's station were two large electronic display screens and a cathode ray tube for data display and an input keyboard.

———————

It was a magnificent aircraft concept in every aspect, but the time was coming that its many critics would win out and have the program stopped.

B-1 Chronology
(B-1A)

1961
Air Force undertook first formal exploratory studies on new generation of aircraft, called SLAB (Subsonic Low Altitude Bomber).

1963
Air Force expended effort with two new studies, ERSA (Extended Range Strategic Aircraft) and LAMP (Low Altitude Manned Penetrator). A number of aerospace companies undertook other studies under government contract including AMP (Advanced Manned Penetrator) and AMPSS (Advanced Manned Penetrating Strategic System).

1965
Four-year AMSA (Advanced Manned Strategic Aircraft) studies, funded by Air Force, undertaken by a number of aerospace companies as a follow-on to industry/Air Force efforts.

1967
Beginning of B-1 contract definition (DSARC I) (1 July).

1969
Formal industry competition began as Air

Force issues Request for Proposal for B-1 (December).

1970
DSARC II completed (4 June) Full Scale Development.

1970
Rockwell International selected as B-1 system contractor; General Electric selected to build engines (June).

1970
Congress approves DOD B-1 funding request of $180.2 million for FY 1970-71.

1971
Congress approves DOD B-1 funding request of $370.3 million for FY 1972.

1971
Full-scale B-1 engineering mockup completed and approved (October/November).

1972
Air Force selects Boeing to integrate B-1 offensive avionics (April).

1972
Congress approves DOD B-1 funding request of $444.5 million for FY 1973.

1973
Congress approves $448.5 million of DOD's $473.5 million B-1 funding request for FY 1974.

1973
Construction starts on first B-1 (flying and handling qualities aircraft).

1974
Air Force selects AIL (Div. of Cutler-Hammer) to develop B-1 defensive avionics (January).

1974
General Electric completed Preliminary Flight Rating Test (PFRT), which was required before the engine could be cleared for flight testing (March).

1974
Design Verification TEST I (DVT I) (Static testing) completed on aft fuselage and flaps (April).

1974
DVT I completed on slats (June).

1974
DVT I completed on nacelle support beam (November).

1974
Rollout of first B-1 at Palmdale, CA (Oct. 26).

1974
Congress approves $445.0 million to DOD's $449.0 million B-1 funding request for FY 1975.

1974
First flight of B-1 from Palmdale, Calif., to Edwards AFB, Calif. (December 23).

1975
B-1 makes first supersonic flight on sixth test flight (April 10).

1975
DVT I on wing-carry-through structure (April).

1975
Full scale static/strength and proof loads test completed on B-1 #2 (July).

1975
General Electric completed Critical Design Review on F101 engine (July).

1975
Full scale static/strength and proof loads test completed on engine nacelle (October).

1975
DVT II (fatigue testing) equaling four lifetimes completed on flaps (October).

1975
Congress approves $813.2 million of DOD's $948.5 million B-1 funding request for FY 1976

& 7T (15-month period). Included in funding total is $87 million for long-lead engineering effort and material for first three operational aircraft. Congress also authorizes startup effort on fourth B-1 prototype (defensive avionics aircraft).

1976
DVT II equaling four lifetimes completed on spoilers (February).

1976
No. 3 B-1 (offensive avionics test aircraft) rolls out (January 16) and makes first flight (April).

1976
DVT II equaling four lifetimes completed on slats (April).

1976
No. 2 B-1 (structural test aircraft) rolls out (May 11) and makes first flight on June 14.

1976
DVT II equaling four lifetimes completed on nacelle support beam (June).

1976
DVT II equaling two lifetimes completed on aft fuselage (August).

1976
Congress approves DOD's $1.53 million B-1 funding request for FY 1977. Of these monies, approximately $1.05 billion is for construction of the first three operational aircraft and long lead engineering effort and material for the next block of eight operational aircraft. Approximately $500 million is for continuing the R&D effort and continuing the work on the fourth prototype. (Congress placed a spending ceiling of $87 million per month on the program through February 1, 1977).

1976
Initial Operational Test & Evaluation (IOT&E) missions, simulating SAC combat missions, successfully completed (September).

1976
Initial flight testing successfully completed

and all test objectives met (September 30).

1976
DVT II equaling two lifetimes completed on wing carry-through structure (November).

1976
General Electric completes Product Verification Program (PV), which consisted of more than 100 separate tests and analyses, includ-ing a 314 hour endurance test that is directly related to B-1 operational missions (November).

1976
Completion of DSARC III, B-1 Production Decision (1 December).

1977
Program cancelled by President Carter.

Chapter III

DEATH AND REBIRTH

It started out like any other Presidential Press Conference. Then President Carter stepped up to the microphone on the 30th of June, 1977, and sounded the death knells on the B-1 program.

The words left no doubt on the immediate future of the exotic bomber program. It seemed as though the magnificent aircraft was just never going to come to be.

"This has been one of the most difficult decisions that I have made since I have been in office," Carter explained. "During the last few months, I have done my best to assess all the factors involving production of the B-1 bomber. My decision is that we should not continue with deployment of the B-1, and I am directing that we discontinue plans for production of this weapons system."

Carter continued that the testing and development program that was already underway should continue in order to provide the needed technical base "in the unlikely event that more cost-effective alternative systems should run into difficulty."

The American Commander-In-Chief further explained that the evolution of the air-launched cruise missile had been one of the main reasons for the dissolution of the B-1 program. He also explained that the continued ability of the B-52 fleet, particularly the G and H models, along with submarine-launched and intercontinental ballistic missiles, provided adequate defense for the nation in his opinion.

The President left the door open, though, for possible future reactivation of the wide-ranging program. He spoke of the problems with the arms negotiations with the Soviets. "…and if at the end of a few years the relations with the Soviet Union should deteriorate drastically, which I don't anticipate, then it may be necessary for me to change my mind. But I don't expect that to happen."

A press release from then-Secretary of Defense Harold Brown followed shortly thereafter, indicating that he had recommended the termination of the program to the President. Brown explained, "The cruise missile option is less expensive. Putting cruise missiles on B-52 launching platforms can take place as early as the beginning of the 1980s—the same time frame as had been planned for the B-1 deployment."

But in all honesty, the B-1 cancellation didn't come as any great surprise to government officials in the know. The bomber had been the subject of great controversy all through the mid-1970s. In fact, in early 1975, the Air Force had been challenged by Congress to prove the need for the new manned bomber or lose the B-1 at that particular time.

That challenge came from Senator Thomas McIntyre, who questioned the need for the expensive program. It was realized at that time that if the Pentagon couldn't convince Congress that the B-1 was essential for U.S. defense, continuation of the program could be in serious jeopardy.

The so-called Joint Strategic Bomber Study, which was generated during that time period, attempted to present the Defense Department's views on the program. But the study was accused by many as being very biased in its views.

Objections to the conclusions were based on several of the ground rules used in the study:

- The study excluded from consideration a surprise Soviet attack.
- The study failed to analyze the long-range interceptor threat.
- But most importantly to questioning Congressmen, the Air Force domination of the group conducting the study undercut its credibility.

Inflation, the nemesis of all major weapons systems, also had plagued the B-1 program from the time the initial contract was awarded in 1970. The estimated cost of building the projected 241 planes had ballooned, for example, from 9.8 billion dollars to more than 13 billion in only four years. Estimates had the program reaching 15 billion for the planned completion of the program in the mid-1980s.

Even in 1974, the General Accounting Office (GAO) criticized the program's rising costs. That watchdog organization recommended to Congress that the Air Force should consider again the long-discussed alternatives of modernizing the B-52 fleet or the FB-111 stretch concept.

Realizing that B-1 costs were going to be a sore point in Congressional circles, the Air Force cut the flight test program from five to three flying models, theoretically saving about three hundred million dollars. (There would eventually be four flying prototypes as the first production aircraft—after the program was cancelled—would be completed and used as a flight test aircraft.)

Also, the target date for a B-1 production decision was shifted six months after the first flight to one year later. Contract awards for the complex avionics equipment were delayed for two years, and scaled back to save another $300 million.

A major cost-cutting maneuver took place when the Air Force decided to reduce by nearly 50 percent the amount of titanium in the aircraft's structure. Numerous other cost-trimming ideas were considered, including the abolishment of the complicated swing wing configuration. That plan—which would not be adopted—considered fixing the wing in some intermediate (i.e., 45 degrees) position.

In mid-1973, the Air Force had also stretched the development schedule in order to help Rockwell through the assembling of the first aircraft. Then another study—there were lots of studies on the B-1—by the National Science Foundation—was authorized "to see how things were going with the B-1 Program."

Details of the aborted crew escape capsule are shown in this early mockup of the system. The stationary rocket would boost the capsule away from the B-1; the gimballed rocket would put the capsule in a level attitude while the winglike fans and spoiler would deploy from their storage areas to stabilize the flying lifeboat until the parachute system opened. (North American Rockwell photo)

The crew escape capsule was tested on a rocket sled at Holloman AFB, New Mexico, beginning in 1972. The test article shown here duplicated the original in shape and weight. The tests showed that the capsule would be ineffective above 350 miles per hour. (North American Rockwell photo)

The report was not encouraging. Performance and range shortcomings were noted, but no major technical problems were uncovered that could have precluded the plane from reaching a production status. Not surprisingly, a morale problem at the Rockwell facility—owing to the uncertainty of the program—was considered to be a serious problem by the study.

One very expensive portion of the aircraft, though, was dropped in 1974—more due to technical problems than to cost considerations. The crew escape module was scrapped in favor of the more conventional, and proven, individual ejection seats.

Tests had shown that the module was ineffective at speeds above 350 miles per hour. To use the system, the aircraft would have had to be slowed to that speed before the crew could eject. It was a situation that obviously could not be tolerated.

Another point of view was brought up on the troubled system one year before its death by Representative Les Aspin of Wisconsin. His was that "the Air Force could have saved between ten and thirty percent of the plane's cost by eliminating the new jet bomber's ability to fly at supersonic speeds."

Quoting from another GAO report, Aspin said "that despite the higher cost of supersonic flight capability, the B-1 will rarely, if ever, fly a supersonic mission. The Air Force has missed a golden opportunity to save the taxpayers as much as $636 million of the program's cost," Aspin asserted.

Aspin said that bombers like the B-1 and B-52 must fly low to avoid the radars and missile defenses of the Soviet Union. "But it is impossible (aerodynamically) technically for a bomber to fly at a low altitude and at supersonic speed. The plane would literally tear itself apart flying above the speed of sound at low altitudes," he added.

The Air Force did make one design change in 1974 that cut the maximum design speed of

The first wind tunnel tests of the B-1's ejection seat were performed at the Arnold Center in 1977. The ejection seat replaced the crew capsule when the latter was found to be unstable at speeds above 350 mph. High-pressure air was used to simulate both the catapult and vernier rocket engines that separate the seat from the aircraft and stabilize it prior to parachute deployment. (U.S. Air Force photo)

the aircraft, but the plane still retained the capability for the craft to fly supersonically. The design change reportedly reduced the cost of the B-1 program by 240 million dollars.

In October of 1974, the first B-1 rolled out the doors of the Palmdale facility, greeting tremendous coverage in all the national magazines and papers. Antiwar groups immediately used the bright white airplane as a symbol of their objections to the entire military scene.

The general thoughts about the plane by government and industry officials were well stated by one observer who commented, "The basic question now is not whether it will fly, but whether we can afford it."

Possibly the biggest opponent to the plane

B-1 number 40169 was the third and last of the B-1 prototypes to roll from the Palmdale Plant 42 facility. Later, the first production aircraft would be added to the fleet after the program was cancelled in 1977. In this photo, the sun is hitting the aircraft's blended fuselage in such a manner that its contours can be clearly seen. (U.S. Air Force photo)

was Senator William Proxmire. The "Golden Fleece Award" Senator made a series of six speeches in 1976 on the B-1, negating the supposed strong points of the sophisticated weapon system.

Proxmire's objections to the system involved the implications of the B-1's supersonic capability, hardening against nuclear blasts, improved takeoff, higher penetration speeds, lower radar image, and larger payloads.

According to Proxmire, "Claims by the manufacturers of the B-1 that it can carry three times the payload of the B-52 are erroneous. While it is true that the B-1 can carry three times more short range attack missiles (SRAMs) internally than the B-52, this is almost meaningless as the B-52 carries an extra twelve SRAMs under its wings and four additional weapons in its forward bomb bay, making a total of 24 weapons per B-52 or the same as the B-1 will carry."

On and on it went, with charges and counter charges being levied for better than half the decade of the 1970s. It finally culminated, of course, with the cancellation of the program in 1977. But as is well known, the B-1 story is far from complete with that initial scrapping of the program.

Immediately, there were questions on what, if anything, would replace the cancelled bomber. The prominent suggestion came from the Air Force in the form of the FB-111H proposal. The program, which was presented to the Committee on Armed Services in September of 1977, proposed "stretching the current FB-111, upgrading its offensive and defensive avionics capabilities, and incorporating the newly-developed B-1 engines."

The proposal was to modify the existing FB-111 aircraft for testing the new subsystems. The aircraft was to be stretched fore and aft of the wing box. The Air Force also indicated that it would restrict the wing sweep to 60 degrees which, with the addition of a fixed inlet, would place the aircraft's performance in the Mach 1.6 speed range at altitude. It was close to that of the cancelled B-1.

Studies continued on various configuration alternatives of the FB-111 stretch proposals, including the examination of B-1 derivative aircraft, and a new bomber aircraft based on the current technology of the time period. The new multi-role aircraft that was to evolve from this research effort was to have an initial operational capability not later than the 1987 time period. The Long-Range Combat Aircraft (LRCA) would have to perform as a conventional iron bomb hauler, a cruise missile launcher, and finally, be able to carry nuclear weapons.

Companies working on the LRCA concept included General Dynamics (FB-111 derivative aircraft), Rockwell (B-1 airframe), Boeing (B-1 offensive avionics), and Airborne Instrument Laboratory (B-1 defensive avionics). In addition, the Air Force was also looking into an advanced technology bomber which would have been powered by a modified version of the GE F101 engine.

Even though President Carter had cancelled production of the B-1 program, the flight testing of the prototypes continued at a steady rate, proving that the system was capable of fulfilling many of its planned-for objectives. Nearly 2000 hours of flight test time were accumulated over the course of the flying program through the late 1970s and into the 1980s with several of the prototypes.

Additional acronyms indicating additional studies began to appear that would serve to shape the capabilities of the follow-on aircraft. Terms such as NTP (Near-Term Penetrator), SWL (Strategic Weapons Launcher), CMCA (Cruise Missile Carrier Aircraft), and MRB (Multi-Role Bomber) were all studies which took place. The follow-on bomber, should it have ever appeared in the future, could have taken many new shapes with a variety of new capabilities.

However, the decision to finally build the B-1B was based largely on results of a Bomber Penetration Study (BPE), another acronym, which was conducted in the late 1970s and

With its wings pulled back in the "supersonic position," this B-1 prototype pours on the coal with fleecy clouds passing by underneath. The forward control fins are clearly visible in this photo. *(U.S. Air Force photo)*

early 1980s, using the original B-1 as the model aircraft. The BPE showed that a combination of smart electronics, tactics, and human resources could defeat the advanced defenses the Soviets were likely to field in the 1990s and beyond. The tests included com-

puterized analysis and flight tests of the B-1 and its avionics systems against predicted Soviet air defense systems.

Shortly thereafter, in October, 1981, the decision was made by President Reagan to fund a fleet of 100 B-1B's (the name of the new plane was appropriate.) The B-1 program—with some sizable improvements and changes in design philosophy—would be resurrected. Thus, in January of 1982, the Air Force awarded contracts for initial development with Rockwell receiving $42 million for aircraft and system integration work. A contract worth 18 million went to Boeing for offensive avionics, the same responsibility the company had possessed with the initial effort. In fact, many of the B-1A (that's what the original B-1 was called) contractors would reacquire their original design and production responsibilities. As another example, Eaton Corporation's AIL Division would again be responsible for the ever-important defensive avionics system. The B-1 program was alive again, a little different and more sophisticated this time around, but alive again.

Learning from the past, costing was a high priority consideration in the early days of the new program. The new B-1B, for example, would share the same shape and structure, for the most part, with the B-1A version. Airframe design shared about 85 percent commonality, while offensive avionics had about a 90 per cent similarity with the advanced systems which had been incorporated in the latter versions of the B-52 bomber. Other offensive systems required few changes from the initial B-1 machine. The new engines for the B-1B were derived directly from those that had rested in the nacelles of the B-1A.

So it was on to the B-1B development program, and hopefully, smoother sailing for the troubled program.

Chapter IV

THE B-1B

Although the B-1B was considered a new aircraft, there would be a considerable amount of the old B-1A retained in the new bird. The B-1B has almost exactly the same dimensions as its older brother, but there is a difference in the performance of the two aircraft.

The high altitude capability of the B-1B has been greatly reduced due primarily to the change of fixed engine inlets from the variable inlets on the B-1A. Also, it was determined that the Mach 2.2 capability was no longer an operational requirement for the aircraft.

Gross takeoff weight of the B-1B was considerably heavier than its precedent (447,000 pounds to 395,000 pounds). Included in that heavier weight is greater payload and more fuel. Additionally, engine thrust of each of the GE F101—GE-102 engines has been slightly increased over the B-1A versions.

Other major changes in the new aircraft include fuel tank provisions in all three weapon bays and a movable bulkhead in the forward two bays to accommodate the Air Launched Cruise Missile. Also, the tail warning system capability has been greatly improved, especially against the air defense missile threat to the plane. The radar cross section of the B-1B has been dramatically reduced. For example, radar image of the B-1A was ten times smaller than that of the B-52. The B-1B has reduced its image to one-tenth that of the B-1A, accomplishing a 100-to-one image reduction over the B-52.

Both offensive and defensive electronics systems are also greatly improved over the original design. Surface wave attenuation materials have also been installed on the wings of the B-1, along with the installation of a low radar cross-section engine inlet using absorbent materials in the vanes of the powerplant. Following is a more detailed look at the different aspects that make up the B-1B.

Structure

An increase of 82,000 pounds caused the B-1B to require considerable airframe strengthening. The changes had to be incorporated in the landing gear, wheels, brakes, and tires, where new demands were imposed. The thousand-pound nose gear cylinder is made of 7175 aluminum while the 3000 pound main gear cylinders are made of low alloy steel.

New materials and processes were also instituted into the structure of the aircraft providing greater strength, lighter weight, and higher reliability than had been possible on the B-1A. Included are the use of composite in bomb bay doors, flaps, and the SMCS vanes for the rotary missile launcher. Also, the B-1B carry-through structure, the major airframe piece to which the wings are attached, is formed through an advanced process called diffusion bonding. In the B-1B, titanium material has been used in this application.

The B-1B can carry up to 14 air launched cruise missiles (ALCM's) or additional fuel along the fuselage. The forward weapons bay was modified to internally carry cruise missiles or fuel. Ejection seats—as opposed to the crew ejection module of the B-1A—are the standard escape system for the B-1B.

Engines

Much of the homework for the B-1B propulsion system had been done by General Electric during the B-1A program and the extensive flight test program that followed. But there were some lessons learned, and some changes to be made. The B-1A flight tests had shown the low altitude terrain-following missions were more severe than expected.

Changes were made in the engine's hot section, while 12 narrow flaps (which eliminated about 85 pounds of weight) replaced eight flaps with seals in the original nozzle section. The new engine also uses scaled components from General Electric's F404 engine that powers the Navy's F/A-18 aircraft.

The B-1B engine features a dual rotor design and has a bypass ratio of 2:1. The augmented turbofan has a low pressure system consisting of a three-stage fan, driven by a two-stage uncooled turbine. The high pressure system, the same as used on the previous engine, consists of a nine-stage axial flow compressor with variable stators, an annular-type combustor, and a single-stage air-cooled turbine.

For augmented operation, fuel is injected into both the fan and core flow paths, providing fully-modulated thrust from minimum to maximum augmentation. The hydraulically-actuated, convergent-divergent nozzle consists of hinged primary and secondary flaps.

B-1 B Fact Sheet

Power Plant:
Four General Electric F101-GE102 turbofan engines (30,000 pounds thrust class)

Maximum Speed:
Low supersonic (high subsonic for low altitude penetration)

Range (Unrefueled)
Intercontinental

Tanker Support:
Compatible with KC-135 and KC-10

Crew:
Four: pilot, co-pilot, and two systems operators (offensive & defensive)

Maximum Operating Weight:
477,000 pounds

Wing Span:
Wings Forward: 137 feet
Wings Swept: 78 feet

Length:
147 feet

Height:
34 feet

VARIABLE SWEEP WING

NO BREAK, LEADING EDGE CONTOUR

"AREA RULED" FUSELAGE

·MIDSHIP, DUALED, UNDERWING NACELLE

BLENDED WING BODY

The B-1B's aerodynamic configuration includes area-ruled fuselage for aerodynamic advantages, blended wing body, and variable sweep wing. Also, there is no break in the leading edge contour of the wing.
(Rockwell International drawing)

B-1B DESIGN FEATURES

- Crew of 4 + 2 instructors

- Ejection seat escape system + bottom bailout

- In-flight refueling

- Heavyweight landing gear

- Wing sweep 15° to 67.5°/3.0g load factor

- Increased weapons carriage versatility

- Upgraded offensive and defensive avionics

- Composite weapons bay doors, SMCS vanes and flaps

- Revised APU start system and added air turbine starters with cross bleed

- Simplified fuel cooling system

- Reduced radar cross section

- Increased nuclear hardening levels

B-1B design features.

(Rockwell International drawing)

COMPARISON

SIZE

B-52

B-1B

PAYLOAD

RADAR CROSS SECTION

B-52

B-1B

Size, payload, and radar signature comparison of B-52 and B-1B.

(Rockwell International drawing)

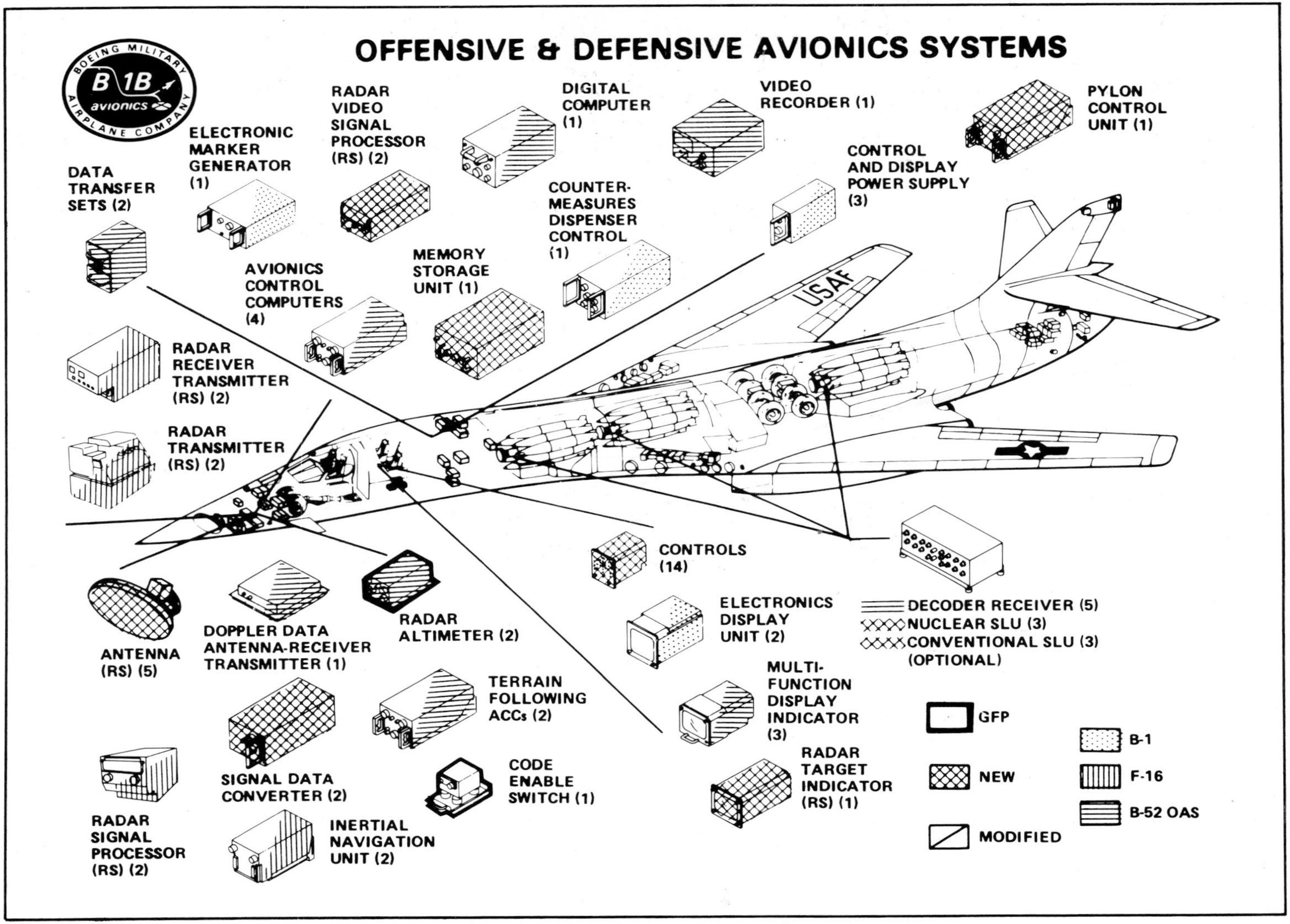

OFFENSIVE & DEFENSIVE AVIONICS SYSTEMS
BOEING MILITARY AIRPLANE COMPANY
B 1B avionics
DATA TRANSFER SETS (2)
ELECTRONIC MARKER GENERATOR (1)
RADAR VIDEO SIGNAL PROCESSOR (RS) (2)
DIGITAL COMPUTER (1)
VIDEO RECORDER (1)
PYLON CONTROL UNIT (1)
CONTROL AND DISPLAY POWER SUPPLY (3)
COUNTER-MEASURES DISPENSER CONTROL (1)
MEMORY STORAGE UNIT (1)
AVIONICS CONTROL COMPUTERS (4)
RADAR RECEIVER TRANSMITTER (RS) (2)
RADAR TRANSMITTER (RS) (2)
USAF
CONTROLS (14)
ANTENNA (RS) (5)
DOPPLER DATA ANTENNA-RECEIVER TRANSMITTER (1)
RADAR ALTIMETER (2)
ELECTRONICS DISPLAY UNIT (2)
DECODER RECEIVER (5)
NUCLEAR SLU (3)
CONVENTIONAL SLU (3) (OPTIONAL)
TERRAIN FOLLOWING ACCs (2)
MULTI-FUNCTION DISPLAY INDICATOR (3)
GFP
SIGNAL DATA CONVERTER (2)
CODE ENABLE SWITCH (1)
RADAR TARGET INDICATOR (RS) (1)
NEW
B-1
F-16
B-52 OAS
MODIFIED
RADAR SIGNAL PROCESSOR (RS) (2)
INERTIAL NAVIGATION UNIT (2)

The vast array of black boxes that constitute the offensive and defensive avionics systems of the B-1B. Note that much of the technology has come from the B-1A program, the F-16, and later electronic modifications to the B-52. (Boeing drawing)

Boeing is developing the offensive avionics system (OAS) for the B-1B, and also providing the controls and displays for both the offensive and defensive operators' stations (mockup shown here). Significant technology improvements in both avionics hardware and software will provide this multi-role aircraft with the most advanced performance capability. Improved data is only one aspect that enhances B-1B performance. Optimum operator interface presents information to the crew in its most useful form at the right time. Both offensive and defensive operators are provided three electronic displays similar to a TV screen but with considerably better quality. Both pictorial and written data are presented on these displays. A newly designed integrated keyboard allows the operator to ''talk to'' the system to ask for new or modified information, or command the system to perform a variety of functions. Arrangement of the controls and displays has been tailored to optimize performance and improve crew environment. Computer-driven cathode ray tubes are used to display weapons, system management, navigation, and defense-related data. Prime viewing area can be used for multiple functions while at the same time allowing flexibility for growth when other systems or capabilities are added to the B-1B. (Boeing photo)

Weapons Capability:
Nuclear/Non-nuclear (i.e., SRAM, ALCM, nuclear gravity and conventional)

Avionics Contractors:
Offensive—Boeing
Defensive—AIL/Eaton

Date of Contract Award:
1982

Alert starting the double pair of massive engines is a snap. The first crew member to the mounting ladder flicks a switch on the nose gear that starts two auxiliary power units. The

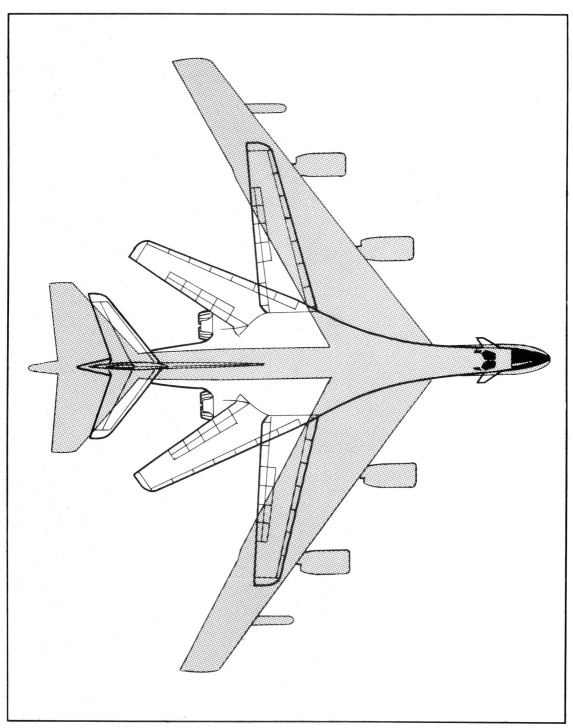

Size comparison between B-1B and B-52 (shaded). Although the B-52's fuselage is only slightly longer than the B-1s, its wingspan is considerably greater.
(Len Pytel drawing)

The original B-1A flying prototypes provided valuable data before the first production B-1Bs could be built. This was the second aircraft built, and the B-1B tail painting was added once the program had been given the go-ahead.
(U.S. Air Force photo)

pilot or co-pilot can then throw four switches that will fire up the engines simultaneously. The engines were designed to be virtually smokeless with the exhaust emissions being considerably lower than most current generation military propulsion systems.

Avionics

Possibly the greatest improvement of the B-1B over the B-1A comes in the avionics area. The offensive avionics include an improved forward-looking/terrain following radar, an improved data bus interface, a highly accurate inertial navigation system, along with the capability to grow when future advancements become available. The new AN/ALQ-161 Defensive Avionics System consists of more than a hundred black boxes which automatically analyze the range of early-warning, ground-controlled intercept, and surveillance and multiple threat radars. Steerable phased-array radars are mounted in the leading edges of the wings and in the tail. In a full jamming mode, the system has been described as putting out above the same power as 120 microwave ovens cooking meals all at the same time.

The offensive avionics for the B-1B are definitely the outgrowth of the original B-1 and the later B-52 systems, along with the addition of proven technological advances. The system provides the capability to readily accept future growth mission requirements including the ALCM armament and conventional stand-off missions.

The B-1B offensive radar system is a multimode, phased array unit based on proven designs employed on the F-16 fighter and other advanced programs. When combined with the BMAC Terrain Following Computers and Radar Data Terminals, it replaces both the Forward Looking and Terrain Following radars used with the B-1A.

The system transmits and receives RF energy through a new phased-array, Low Observable Antenna, which exhibits a much lower radar

cross section than did the three dish antenna configurations used on the original aircraft. The radar system provides greater accuracy for mapping functions, additional operating modes, and decreased possibility of detection by unfriendly radars.

The B-1B inertial navigation system, in a single unit, provides the equivalent functions of the past B-1 system, which consisted of an inertial measurement unit and a separate electronics unit. The B-1B Inertial Measurement System provides greater accuracy over long-term operation to permit the B-1B avionics to meet its more demanding missile and gravity bomb delivery requirements.

The B-1B avionics are controlled by the software in six IBM central computers, two microcomputers, and additional processors in the Inertial Navigation system and Offensive Radar System. The computers are enhancements of the versions used on the B-52 Offensive Avionics System and represent a significant advancement over the system used in the B-1A. These computer and software improvements significantly reduce the life cycle costs for the B-1B while allowing for growth flexibility in the future.

Backup electronic systems were also expanded for the B-1B. Inherent in the avionics management by the software is the continuous monitoring, detection and fault reaction for the avionics equipment. For equipment failures or possible battle damage, the computer programs use backup sensors to maintain the system on-line. With multiple failures, the software locates the best available data so as to enable mission completion.

Additional B-1B advancements are provided in the computational area by the use of a core memory Mass Storage Device in place of the drum storage used on the original B-1 and by use of Data Transfer Units developed for the B-52 Offensive Avionics System (OAS) for data handling. Memory modules in the Mass Storage Device are identical to that in the B-1B processors, thereby minimizing logistics costs.

B-1B stores management functions have advanced greatly over the techniques which were planned for the B-1A system. The newer system has the capability for delivering additional weapon types. The ALCM system, of course, will now be one of the new weapons for the B-1B.

Flight test experience has also improved the operator interface with the avionics system. The testing has resulted in better location of operator controls and displays. B-1B has expanded on the multi-function display concept that the past B-1 and B-52 avionics upgrade programs utilized.

Nuclear Protection

In aircraft before the B-1B, crews had relied on protective goggles for protection against thermonuclear light and heat emission. The B-1B cockpit will be fitted with darkening panels and protective portholes capable of reducing incoming light to 0.003 percent of its original intensity.

The cockpit darkening panels are designed to cover the forward windshield and side windows. The forward windshield panels are attached flush to the top of the instrument panel shroud and are affixed with pushbutton snaps. With the portholes and panels in place, visibility is possible only through the portholes, which permits a 5.5 inch field of view.

Standing like a beacon in the California desert, the B-1 microwave test facility (topped by a scale B-1) was used to verify radar cross-section data.
(U.S. Air Force Photo)

Chapter V

WEAPONS

What good is a high-performance bomber without offensive weapons to carry to the enemy? The aircraft serves basically as a mounting platform for various weapons, with the B-1B being no different. The new bomber is a versatile system with a number of different weapon systems being available.

With the B-1 system having a long development period, including a cancellation and then a later program start-up, the different weapons that have been considered for the bomber have also changed with the times.

During the early 1970s time period, a number of penetration systems had been considered for the new B-1A bomber. One concept called for a short range bomber defense missile to protect the aircraft against hostile defense interceptors. The missile, which would never reach fruition, was to have been radar-guided.

A longer-range version of the SAM defense missile was also considered to defend the plane against air defense missiles at ranges as

great as 250 miles. Finally, a low-altitude penetration missile with B-1A applications was also considered. Like the earlier short-range air defense system, both of these systems would also be cancelled.

Like the Quail decoy missile that was carried by the B-52, a Subsonic Cruise Armed Decoy (SCAD) system was also considered for the B-1A. The program would provide much of the technology for the cruise missile program to follow. The 1,350 pound AGM-86A missile was envisioned as a thousand-mile armed decoy. Turbofan-powered, the vehicle was to carry ECM jammers and decoys designed to simulate radar returns of the launching bomber and to spread confusion among enemy radar systems. It was cancelled by the Air Force in 1973.

But a system which had early roots that wasn't cancelled was the Boeing AGM-69A Short Range Attack Missile (SRAM), which found application with the B-52G and H models along with the FB-111. The missile went into

This Rockwell drawing of the 1980 time period shows the concept for a Strategic Air-Launched Cruise Missile Launcher loaded with AGM-86B missiles. Considerable testing on this configuration was performed at the Air Force's Arnold Engineering Development Center in Tullahoma, Tennessee. *(Rockwell International drawing)*

production in 1970 and the Air Force accepted the first operational SRAM in 1972. The FB-111 was the first aircraft to receive the SRAM, followed by the two latest models of the B-52. Of course, the ultimate goal was to equip the B-1B with the advanced missile system. However, it would be well into the 1980s, on the B-1B, before the mating would take place.

The solid-fueled SRAM has two attack modes, high and low, and once launched it cannot be jammed or deflected, since it has a self-contained inertial guidance. During the high mode, both pulses of the two-pulse rocket motor are burned, giving the missile about three times the range than in the low mode.

Twenty SRAMs can be carried by the B-52, six

on pylons under each wing and eight internally. Six SRAMs are the top load that can be negotiated with the FB-111. The SRAM load for the B-1B (if all of its payload were devoted to that particular system) would be 32. Twenty-four, eight each in three weapons bays, and eight more externally would be the mounting configuration for the B-1 SRAM application.

But the present high-level load to be carried by the B-1B is the Air Launched Cruise Missile. The application of the missile, which had much to do with the cancellation of the B-1 in the first place, became a prime consideration in the late 1970s following the cancellation. During that time period, the Air Force began to evaluate the feasibility of a B-1 type aircraft mated to the cruise missile. Other aircraft evaluated at

1980 cruise missile with a B-1 derivative aircraft showed that the B-1 would be compatible with the ALCM.
(U.S. Air Force photo)

the same time for the cruise missile application included the Boeing 747, Lockheed 1011, and McDonnell Douglas DC-10 commercial transports, and the USAF Lockheed C-5A.

The studies showed that the B-1 was still the best launching platform for the ALCM, all other factors considered. The results weighed heavily on selecting the B-1 follow-on aircraft to continue the U.S. manned bomber program during the 1980s.

Boeing was selected as the contractor for the AGM-86B cruise missile, which went into production in 1981. The B-52 was again the first aircraft to get the new missile with a total of 12 being carried externally in clusters of six on each main underwing pylon. An internal group of eight will bring the total B-52 ALCM capability to 20. The B-1B will be able to carry eight ALCMs internally and 14 externally on pylons under the wing glove. Discussions, though, have indicated that 20 ALCMs might be the maximum B-1B load.

The ALCM itself is an electronic marvel. It is, in effect, a small, extremely versatile, unmanned, self-guided airplane which is capable of electronically reading the terrain over which it flies. It compares these readings with maps stored

The ALCM in an early test flight. Looking somewhat like a small fighter aircraft, the missile uses its sophisticated guidance system to approach the target at a low altitude, under the detection range of enemy radar. *(U.S. Air Force photo)*

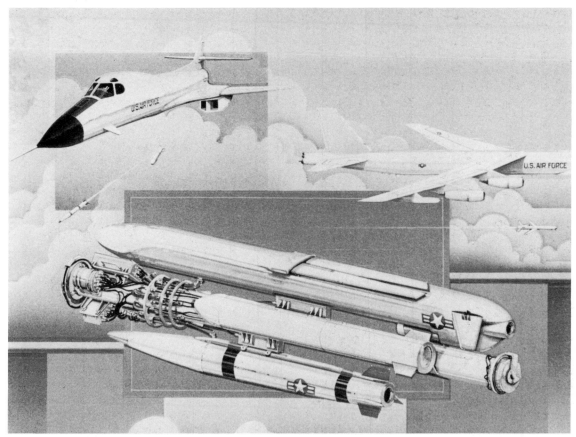

Artist's rendition of the Common Strategic Rotary Launcher (CRSL) being developed for the Air Force by Boeing. The new launcher is compatible with the SRAM and ALCM missiles, along with all the gravity weapons to be deployed on the B-1B. (U.S. Air Force photo)

in its on-board computer, guiding itself through the enemy's defense systems to predetermined targets. The missile is armed with a W-80 nuclear warhead.

The ALCM's range of more than 1,500 miles and small radar cross section gives the Air Force a weapon which can be launched over non-hostile territory and still reach major targets. Weighing one and one-half tons, the AGM-86B measures 20-feet, 9-inches long and has a deployed wingspan of 12-feet.

The ALCM and B-1B will come together for the first time on the 19th production model. In addition to the external mounting possibilities for the ALCM, there will also be the capability

for launching the missiles from an internal installation.

The key to the B-1B ALCM internal installation is the Common Strategic Rotary Launcher (CSRL), which will be compatible with ALCMs, SRAMs, and all gravity free-fall bombs. Any future ALCM versions will also be compatible with the launcher. One such variant being considered for the B-1B is an advanced longer-range ALCM, called the Advanced Cruise Missile (ACM). Boeing will build the launchers, which could well number over 200 by contract completion in 1987. The launchers are being designed expressly for the B-52H and the B-1B.

An earlier version of the rotary launcher was

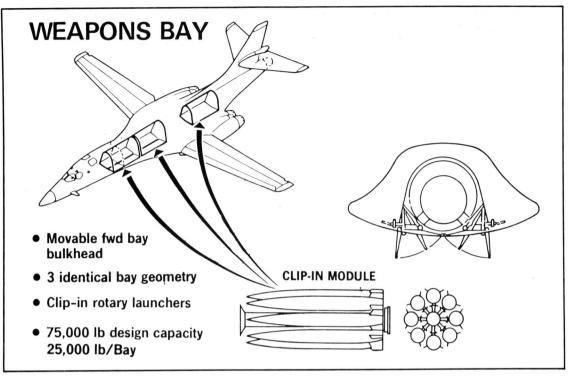

WEAPONS BAY

- **Movable fwd bay bulkhead**
- **3 identical bay geometry**
- **Clip-in rotary launchers**
- **75,000 lb design capacity 25,000 lb/Bay**

CLIP-IN MODULE

B-1B weapons bay.   *(Rockwell International drawing)*

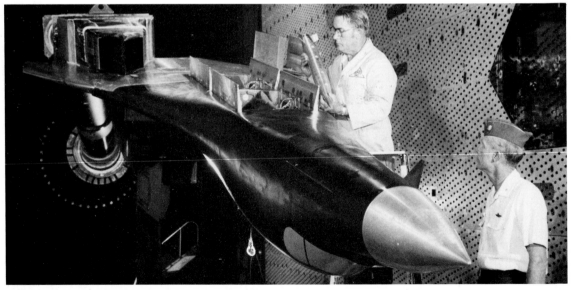

Mapping the sound levels generated in and around the bomb bay of the first B-1 design throughout the transonic range was accomplished at Arnold Engineering Development Center. Here an ARO technician installs a model of the SRAM missile for further aerodynamic testing in 1973. The tests were carried out using a 20 percent model of the aircraft in the center's 16-foot transonic wind tunnel.   *(U.S. Air Force photo)*

CONVENTIONAL STORES COMPARISON
INTERNAL CARRIAGE (WEAPONS BAY)

B-1B			B-52 (1,043 CU FT)			
(1,643 CU FT)			B-52D ONLY*		OTHER B-52'S	
WEAPON	QTY	DROP SPEED (KIAS)	QTY	DROP SPEED** (KIAS)	QTY	DROP SPEED**
MK82GP	84	600	108	390	27	
MK82SE	84	600	84	390		
M117GP	36	600	66	390	27	390 KIAS
M117R	36	600	60	390	27	
B-61	24	600				
MK84	24	600	18	390	8	

* 23% of original production were B-52D's (170)   ** Bomb bay door limitation
32% of remaining aircraft are B-52D's (145)

Conventional stores comparison, internal carriage (weapons bay).   (Rockwell International)

Full-scale B-1 mockup was used for antenna system testing.   (U.S. Air Force Photo)

B-1B WEAPONS VERSATILITY

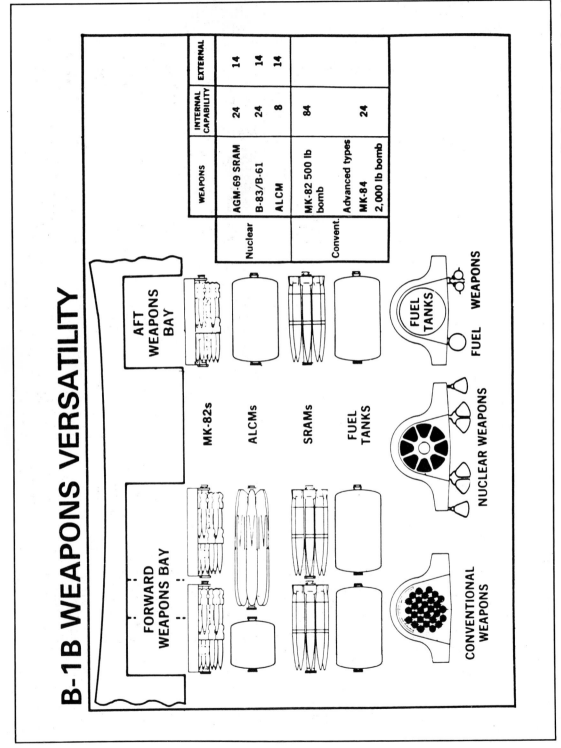

	WEAPONS	INTERNAL CAPABILITY	EXTERNAL
Nuclear	AGM-69 SRAM	24	14
	B-83/B-61	24	14
	ALCM	8	14
Convent.	MK-82 500 lb bomb	84	
	Advanced types MK-84 2,000 lb bomb	24	

AFT WEAPONS BAY

FORWARD WEAPONS BAY

MK-82s

ALCMs

SRAMs

FUEL TANKS

FUEL TANKS

FUEL WEAPONS

NUCLEAR WEAPONS

CONVENTIONAL WEAPONS

(Rockwell International drawing)

B-1B weapons versatility.

The B-52 was equipped with the advanced ALCM system before the B-1B. Here a B-52G bomber is shown carrying its complement of AGM-86B missiles while being refueled by a KC-135 Tanker. The ALCM achieved initial operational capability with the B-52 in December 1982. *(Boeing Company photo)*

The SRAM has long been an operational weapon with the General Dynamics FB-111 system. In this photo, the aircraft is carrying its complement of four SRAMs. The system will be compatible with the B-1B, which will also carry the ALCM among several other weapons. *(Boeing Company photo)*

Chapter VI

FLIGHT TEST

A major portion of the B-1 program has been embodied in its extensive flight test program. And as had been the case with all other aspects of the program, the flight testing evolved into several different phases.

The first portion of the testing began on December 23, 1974, when B-1 prototype number one took to the air from Air Force Plant 42 at Palmdale and landed at Edwards Air Force Base. It would later be followed by two other aircraft during this period, each of which would have specific mission roles during their test periods. The overall mission of the testing, though, was to support the planned production of the B-1 in the late 1970s.

The aircraft were configured as follows:

    B-1 Number One (40158)—flying qualities
      and performance
    B-1 Number Two (40159)—structural loads
    B-1 Number Three (40160)—offensive
      avionics

During the first phase, the prototypes accomplished a number of significant milestones including many hours of Mach one plus speeds and a top speed of approximately Mach 2.2.

The end of the first phase and the start of the second was brought about by the cancellation of the B-1 production program. Fortunately, though, the flight test portion of the program was retained for research and development.

The reported purpose of the continuation of flight testing was "to support development of the B-1's advanced subsystems, particularly the electronic countermeasures systems." Remaining tasks which were also accomplished included penetration of simulated enemy defenses, defensive avionics testing, and development and integration of the sophisticated defensive systems.

It was during this interim that a fourth member was added to the B-1 prototype fleet. At the time of the B-1 cancellation, the first B-1 production aircraft was so near completion that the decision was made to complete the aircraft and make it a part of the flight testing. It first flew in 1979, and would become an important part of the B-1B testing program in the 1980s.

This interim and test period lasted for four years, with the last flights of prototypes 3 and 4 occurring in April 1981. At that time they joined the first two aircraft in storage at Edwards. In all, the four planes had completed 347 flights and recorded 1,895.2 flight hours without incident. No one was sure when those last flights took place whether the majestic birds would ever fly again, or eventually be shuttled off to museums across the country at some future date.

The final mission of the two prototypes was to support the earlier mentioned Bomber Penetration Evaluation Study that was being accomplished during that time period by Boeing and Rockwell-International. Little did anybody know at the time that the results of those studies would show that a B-1 type aircraft was still the best approach to meet the bomber requirements of the nation.

Once that decision was made in 1981, new life again brewed for the fleet (at least for two of them), and a restart of flight testing was begun. From supporting B-1A production to research and development, to storage, to finally supporting B-1B production—a weird trail through the years had been woven by the prototype.

The final flight testing period was based on three aircraft original prototypes 2 and 4 plus the first B-1B of the Rockwell assembly line in Palmdale. The number 2 prototype was planned to test and evaluate weapons carriage and separation characteristics, and confirm flight control modifications and flying qualities. The long-since-cancelled escape capsule was retained in the aircraft. In the original B-1 program, that particular aircraft had logged more than 282 hours on 60 flights. It also achieved the top speed of the four aircraft, the Mach 2.22 figure on October 5, 1978. It will also be modified with weapons hard-points and an

internal cruise missile rotary launcher. The aircraft was also planned for testing the B-1's capability to fly in a "three-engine out" configuration. One of the last, and certainly most important jobs, of prototype number 2 is to test the release and free fall characteristics of 500 pound Mk 82 bomb, the B-61 and B-83 nuclear free fall weapons, and the Mk 30 DST sea mine.

Prototype number 4, flown to and displayed at the 1982 Farnborough International Air Show in England, was planned for testing the B-1B's offensive and defensive avionics sytems and verify them for operational use. That aircraft started its test period in 1984. The #4 test period was planned for some 380 hours of flight time which could push its use into mid-June 1986.

The first production B-1B is scheduled to enter the reactivated test program in 1985, and will be tested and evaluated at the "full capability" B-1B prior to introduction of the bomber into the Strategic Air Command inventory beginning in 1986.

Those were the plans until August 29, 1984, when prototype number 2 crashed while conducting a low-speed stability and control test. Killed was Rockwell Chief Test Pilot T. D. (Doug) Benefield, while Major Richard Reynolds and Captain Otto Waniczek were injured. The three crew members ejected in the crew escape capsule.

Ironically, the crash occurred just a few days before the official roll-out of the first B-1B production aircraft (September 4) at the Palmdale production plant. Statements at that event indicated that the program would not be appreciably affected by the crash.

But obviously, loss of the heavily-instrumented number 2 aircraft would affect the remaining portions of the flight test program. Preliminary plans called for the ALCM separations tests—which had been programmed for the number 2 plane—to be accomplished by the ninth pro-

Elaborate wind tunnel testing was accomplished on many B-1 models. (U.S. Air Force photo)

duction aircraft. The 10th production B-1B would be used to supplement the ALCM test program if necessary.

Also, the number 4 prototype was temporarily grounded following the accident, but it was expected to continue its programmed test program functions following the crash investigation.

The first of the B-1A prototypes takes shape at the Rockwell Palmdale facility. The aircraft would be flown extensively in the flight test program at Edwards Air Force Base, California. *(U.S. Air Force photo)*

A view in the early 1970s of the Los Angeles operation of North American Rockwell in the fabrication of the crew escape modules for the first B-1 models. In the background are completed modules. The concept would later be dropped when it was determined that the escape technique was unsafe above 350 mph. The escape mode for the B-1 was changed to the standard ejection seat technique. (North American Rockwell photo)

Prototype number two, with its European One camouflage shining in the California sun, takes to the air in a summer 1984 test flight. (U.S. Air Force photo)

B-1A prototype number two with wings nearly in full-forward position on a mid-1984 test flight.   (U.S. Air Force photo)

In mid-1984, B-1A prototype number two received the European One paint scheme. The job was performed by a crew from Tinker Air Force Base and was accomplished on the ramp at Edwards.   (U.S. Air Force photo)

Looking rough and ready, B-1A prototype number two displays its new European One camouflage. (U.S. Air Force photo)

One requirement of the B-1 bomber is a significant low-altitude capability. This prototype demonstrates that capability low over the California desert in an early 1970s flight test. *(U.S. Air Force photo)*

Then Security of Defense Melvin Laird gets a firsthand look at the B-1 simulator, which would be used by B-1 pilots before their first actual flight. The simulator was linked to computers that afforded the pilots all the feel of the B-1's aerodynamic maneuvers—climbing, descending, pitch, roll, and yaw. An earlier simulator had permitted only "blind" instrument flying. The simulator allowed pilots to "fly" several hundred hours in the B-1 before reaching the actual aircraft. (North American Rockwell photo)

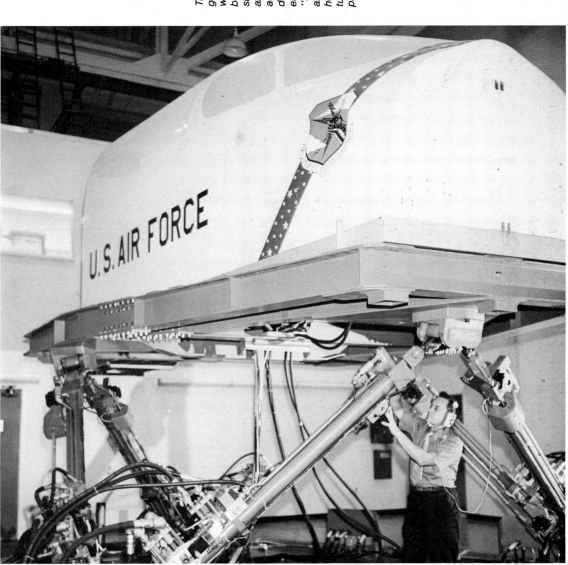

The number four B-1A prototype—in effect, the first production aircraft—stands ready at Edwards Air Force Base. Yes, that white stuff stacked about is snow! (U.S. Air Force photo)

B-1A prototype number two (shown here) and four will be heavily involved in the B-1B production phase. The number two prototype will be used for stability and control testing, along with weapons verifications. (U.S. Air Force photo)

The number three B-1 B-1A prototype was the first of the fleet to receive camouflage paint. This would be the only aircraft, though, to receive this particular desert ("Asia Minor") scheme. The later European One scheme would eventually be adopted as standard. (U.S. Air Force photo)

B-1A number three prototype in desert camouflage. (U.S. Air Force photo)

Chapter VII

PRODUCTION AND DEPLOYMENT

The goal of the B-1B production program is quite simple: Equip the Strategic Air Command with 100 aircraft (down considerably from the 241 of the original B-1A models) at a projected budget cost of $20.5 billion in 1981 dollars. The unit fly-away cost of each aircraft is $187.1 million.

Through its stormy military and political past, the aircraft has emerged in a production state with an advanced management system to produce the exceptionally complex aircraft.

Starting with the first production aircraft in late 1984, the new Rockwell assembly building would serve as the production site for all 100 of the majestic craft. The new-for-the-job facility was formally opened in November 1983, and encompasses nearly one million square feet which pushed the prime contractor's total square footage devoted to the B-1B to some 7.5 million square feet.

Ground was broken for the "bomber building" in

March 1982, and includes the following different areas:

- A 422,000-square foot final assembly building where the mating of major B-1B structures takes place.
- A 254,000-square foot checkout building in which the aircraft's systems are final tested before flight operations and delivery to the Air Force.
- A 256,000-square foot tubing and electrical harness building which will support final assembly operations.

In all, the building cost $100 million dollars to construct.

But the assembly building was only a small part of the total $400 million investment by Rockwell for the B-1B program. That facility supplemented existing B-1B facilities operated by Rockwell at nearby Air Force Plant 42, which produced the forward fuselage. This particular building was the

Rollout for the wing carry-through structure for the first B-1B. The work is being accomplished at Rockwell's Columbus, Ohio facility. The carry-through also serves to carry fuel. Note the ''lobes'' for attachment of pins for the swing wing.
(Rockwell International photo)

Rockwell technicians install wing pins and nacelles on the first B-1B at Rockwell's final assembly facility in Palmdale.
(Rockwell International photo)

Forward fuselage section of second B-1B in Rockwell's forward fuselage assembly plant at Palmdale.

(Rockwell International photo)

The B-1B wing carry-through structure is moved about the Rockwell plant in Columbus, Ohio. (Rockwell International photo)

The B-1B wing installation process is carried out at the B-1 final assembly facility in Palmdale. Also note the installation of the engine nacelles. (Rockwell International photo)

B-1B MAJOR SECTIONS AND SUBSYSTEMS

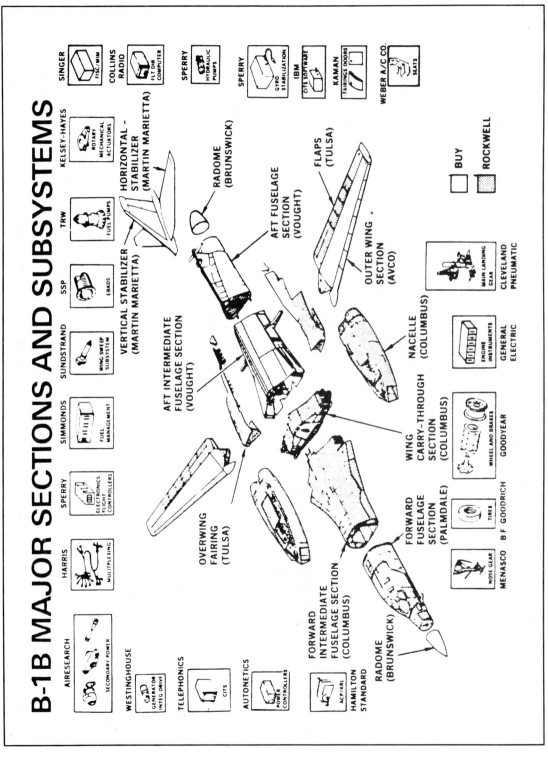

B-1B major sections and subsystems.

(Rockwell International drawing)

The B-1B number one aircraft is starting to take shape in this early 1984 photo. The work is being done at the Rockwell Palmdale facility for scheduled September 1984 rollout. (Rockwell International photo)

The first production B-1B under test in the Automated Test Facility. Tests of the aircraft's electrical, cooling, pneumatic, fuel, and hydraulic systems were carried out in mid-1984. Following completion of the testing, this aircraft joined the other B-1A prototypes in the continuing flight test program. *(U.S. Air Force photo)*

location of final assembly for the B-1A.

At the peak of the B-1B program, which is projected to be in the 1986-87 time period, Rockwell would employ approximately 4,600 persons at the company facilities and at Edwards Air Force Base.

The assembly operation for the B-1B begins in the large assembly building with the attachment of the vertical stabilizer to the aft fuselage section. The five fuselage sections are actually mated by placing the five-foot-long wing carry-through

section on a fixed mating stand. Serving as the center section of the fuselage, the carry-through structure has pivots for the swing wings, which are later attached to the aircraft.

The next portion of the production process involves the mating of the aft intermediate fuselage. This fuselage section includes the attachments for the main landing gear and one of the weapons bays. It is mated to the rear end of the carry-through structure. The two forward weapons bays are contained in the forward intermediate section, which is mated to the opposite end of the carry-

A head-on view of the first production B-1B. The blended fuselage of the aircraft design is clearly in this photo. Obviously, the aircraft has not received its final paint scheme in this portion of the checkout program.　　　(U.S. Air Force photo)

through structure. Finally, the forward section and the aft fuselage section are attached to the intermediate sections, completing the five-piece joining operation.

A production change between the B-1A and B-1B occurred with the addition of a movable, non-load-bearing bulkhead in the B version. Beginning with aircraft number nine, the device will be moved forward such that cruise missiles can be accommodated in the second weapons bay. The first eight aircraft would be retrofitted later to accept the ALCM. The ninth production aircraft will be the test aircraft for the ALCM program in 1986 and 1987. Following the assembly of the five fu-

selage sections, the aircraft is then integrated with its vertical stabilizer, nacelles, horizontal stabilizers, radomes, and finally, its swing wings.

The next stop is where the GE engines are installed, along with the main landing gear doors and fairings. Finally, the completed B-1B is moved to a nearby checkout facility where complete hydraulic, electrical, fuel, pneumatic and avionics tests are performed. Then, as a last step, the plane receives its grey-and-green camouflage paint scheme.

The rate of production is expected to initially start at about one aircraft per month, but to have in-

Forward intermediate fuselage for second B-1B after mating of the top deck at the Rockwell Palmdale facility.
(U.S. Air Force photo)

A B-1B wing assembly is prepared at Avco Corporation's Nashville, Tennessee, plant. Note the "lobe" for attachment of the pin, which gives the B-1B its swing-wing capability.
(Avco photo)

The first production B-1B undergoing checkout following its completion. The photo was taken during June 1984. (U.S. Air Force photo)

The first production B-1B is rolled from the final assembly building at Palmdale to the nearby systems test building. (U.S. Air Force photo)

creased to about one per week by the time the 23rd aircraft had been reached. When the full production rate of four per month is reached, the assembly of a B-1B is expected to take about nine weeks, while the strenuous checkout of the aircraft could require about three weeks additional time.

The production schedule calls for the 100th aircraft to be delivered by the spring of 1988. Two bombers will be based at Edwards AFB, California, for continued flight test. Four aircraft will be delivered to SAC in 1985, 32 in 1986, 48 in 1987, and the final 14 in 1988.

Deployment

Long before the first production B-1B rolled off the end of the production line, the Air Force was formulating where the advanced aircraft would be deployed.

The planning actually started in August 1983 with the activation of ASD Detachment 20 at Dyess Air Force Base, Texas. The organization had the important duty of managing the B-1B start-up activities at the base, the first to receive the new bomber.

Located near Abilene, Texas, Dyess AFB took delivery of its first B-1B in June 1985, and should reach initial operational capability with a full squadron of 16 bombers in the fall of 1986. Dyess would also be the site of SAC's Combat Crew Training Squadron, which will include 19 additional B-1Bs.

By February 1984, plans for the remaining B-1B deployment had been made. Ellsworth Air Force Base, South Dakota; Grand Forks Air Force Base, North Dakota; and McConnell Air Force Base, Kansas, would be the additional three bases to get the B-1B. The introduction of the new aircraft also cause B-52 and KC-135 aircraft to be shifted around to other bases.

Beginning in late 1986, Ellsworth AFB will start receipt of 32 B-1Bs. Nineteen existing B-52H aircraft would be transferred elsewhere. The following year, Grand Forks AFB will convert from 16 B-52Gs to 19 B-1Bs. Deployment at McConnell AFB begins in 1988 when the first of its B-1Bs is received.

Chapter VIII

THE FUTURE

With production well underway in the 1984 time period, it would have appeared the future of the B-1B was intact, but that just hasn't been the name of the game with this system. During its 15 years of development the B-1 had faced many challenges, and during the early 1980s it started to face another.

It is called the "Stealth" bomber program, and its exotic technology, which has a way of greatly lessening the radar cross section of an aircraft on enemy radar screens, was in an R&D stage with the Northrop Corporation. Whether the technology would ever be incorporated into an active aircraft program was uncertain at this time.

And that's where the debate began. Many Congressmen argued that the B-1B would be an obsolete aircraft by the time it reached operational status because of the Stealth technology that might be available at that time. In fact, in 1983, a vote was held on the Senate floor to examine just how much power the Stealth concept actually

had. The vote was on whether to kill the B-1B and instead approve a crash program to develop a stealth bomber. Fortunately for the B-1B, the move failed by the rather decisive vote of 68 to 30.

During 1984, some individuals outside the Air Force suggested a compromise alternative between the two advanced concepts. The suggestion was to incorporate the Stealth technology into the B-1B, and possibly produce a second batch of 100 Stealth B-1s. Those would be called B-1C.

It has been argued that this approach would be considerably cheaper than developing a completely new stealth aircraft concept. It has also been argued that another hundred B-1s could be bought from continuing production at half the $20 billion cost of the first hundred aircraft.

So, as this book goes to press, there are still uncertainties on where the B-1B will finally evolve. The alternatives seem endless: (1) completed production of the programmed 100 aircraft and

Visual refueling aid in the form of painted stripes was added to one of the test aircraft for evaluation. (U.S. Air Force photo)

then cession of production; (2) production halted by a change in direction toward Stealth technology or by another administration; (3) continued production of the B-1B in its present configuration beyond the currently projected production run; (4) continued production of the aircraft beyond the 100 aircraft goal in a reconfigured B-1C configuration.

However, Air Force Vice Chief of Staff General Lawrence Skantze in February 1984 made clear the Air Force position on that matter. The General confirmed that at that time the Air Force was still considering the B-1B and the Stealth bomber programs as separate programs.

As history has shown, though, it all remains to be seen. But there is one thing for certain: Whatever its ultimate future, the B-1B will always be regarded as the most sophisticated manned bomber every built by this country—or for that matter, any country.

The B-1B could well be the last of an era in modern warfare—the last of the manned bombers!

INDEX